# HE SAID, SHE SAID

## BILL & ANABEL GILLHAM

**HARVEST HOUSE PUBLISHERS**
Eugene, Oregon 97402

HE SAID, SHE SAID

Copyright © 1995 by Harvest House Publishers
Eugene, Oregon 97402

Library of Congress Cataloging-in-Publication Data
Gillham, Bill.
    He said, she said / Bill and Anabel Gillham.
      p.   cm.
    Includes bibliographical references.
    ISBN 1-56507-254-5
    1. Marriage—Religious aspects—Christianity.     I. Gillham,
Anabel.  II. Title.
BV835.G543   1995
248.8'44—dc20                          94-37964
                                           CIP

*To the Marriage Maker,*
*the Essence of Our Oneness*

# ACKNOWLEDGMENTS

We give our thanks to those God has called to be an integral part of our ministry as encouragers, supporters, and dear brothers and sisters. Because you have loved us and shared your lives with us, we have grown in our capacity for understanding, for compassion, and for consecration to persevere in the role God has given to us.

We would like to give a special word of thanks to our son, Will Gillham, whose editing proved invaluable.

# FOREWORD

Three important elements converge in this book, making it unique. The first and foremost quality of the Gillham's ministry is a belief that biblical instruction is not only for salvation of our souls, but also for our lives. Each partner in a marriage is first a unique creation of God; since He made us, He alone can fix us and make us able to function as whole people in a marriage.

The second element of this book is the extensive experience that Bill and Anabel have had with actual people in real marriages. So very much of what we believe about normalcy in marriage today has been gained through the media. Here the situations often are not the creations of real life or of God, but are the arbitrary concoctions of a novelist or playwright playing God, often weaving into the characters their own personal struggles, wishful thinking, angers, responses, and a host of social theory not yet accepted by most of society.

Bill and Anabel deal daily with real people who have built into their lives the values, presuppositions, struggles, and needs that are their own and therefore must be dealt with by a return to the basics. And for the Christian that means: How does my behavior mesh with God's will and the role He gave me in the world? At the root, this book argues for faith that expresses itself in submission to the creative wisdom of our Creator, who thought up the whole idea of male and female, sexuality, marriage, children, family, and human diversity.

Finally, there is the truly empathetic tone that comes through as two very different people, Bill and Anabel, with disarming transparency give us an intimate look into their personal growth process and the practical lessons that have helped them through their daily challenges. They do not suggest a state of bliss where no problems exist but more realistically help us see the source of our pain and then present us with ways that we can act to solve our conflicts and struggles.

As I read this manuscript, I kept saying to myself, *I want my own kids to read this—this book will help any marriage.*

—Jay Kesler

# TABLE OF CONTENTS

# CHRIST IN US, THE HOPE...

*Your new birth in Christ
gave you a new identity—your
true identity now and
throughout all eternity.*

# — Chapter One —

There must be hundreds of good books and seminars on the subject of marriage. Why should we write another one? Is there some dramatic new discovery which will turn a sour marriage into a sweet one? Something that can transform a good one into a great one? Yes—we believe there is. Our "discovery" is as old as the New Testament. Yet to the Christian who has not yet grasped it, the idea will seem new.

We're talking about the "mystery" of which Paul wrote in his letter to the Colossians. As husband and wife, we're the first to admit that we've been unable to make our own marriage succeed. But we have learned that Christ, living through us, is not only able to make marriage work, but work beautifully.

> *Our discovery for miraculously improving marriage—and every other aspect of our lives— is allowing Christ to "life out" our daily existence through us.*

## "Doing Our Best—With God's Help"

Agape love is *active*; it is doing the most constructive, edifying, redemptive thing possible for your spouse. However, thousands of believers have found out that they simply cannot live out a consistent, agape-love lifestyle with their spouses. They know how marriage is supposed to work, but they can't seem to make it happen.

Most Christian husbands and wives are trying to "do their best with God's help," either because they have never been exposed to the reality of the biblical method (faith in Christ to do it all through you) or because they do not understand how to practically apply it. Perhaps by now your own failure has prepared you, through the Holy Spirit, for the one strategic answer you'll find in this book. That answer which the Bible calls "the mystery" is: "Christ *in* you, the hope of glory" (Colossians 1:27). When it comes to troubled marriages, Christ is always the missing ingredient. It's simply a matter of understanding how to cooperate with Him so He can freely work through each of you.

## Two Roads, Not Three

Married or single, young or old, there are only two ways a Christian can operate (the Bible calls it *walking*): he can walk "in the Spirit," or he can walk "after the flesh." Unfortunately, some of us have assumed that there are three ways to live, and we've defined our alternatives something like this:

- "In the Spirit" meant teaching Sunday School and helping little old ladies cross the street.
- "After the flesh" meant lusting after the opposite sex, or after various other worldly attractions.
- "My way" is our idea of a third option. This involves my work-a-day world—eating, sleeping, playing with the kids, watching ball games, etc.—all of which we consider neither sinful nor spiritual.

The problem is, the Bible says nothing about a third way. It speaks only of two ways, "in the Spirit" and "after the flesh." And the Bible's definitions are quite different than ours: "In the Spirit" means trusting in the "Spirit of Christ" (the Holy Spirit) to express His obedient, agape Life through us. "After the flesh" means trusting in our own strength, talent, skills, resources, patterns for living, street smarts, and whatever else we can come up with, to carry us through the day (see Philippians 3:3-9).

Satan, the deceiver, wants Christians to live lives which bring dishonor to the reputation of Jesus Christ. God's plan for us, on the other hand, is that our lives bring honor to Christ. The Christian who allows Christ to live through him is going to bring honor to Him. The one who trusts in his own flesh is not going to experience victory over the world, the flesh, and the devil, and will dishonor Christ. The responsibility for making moment-by-moment choices between those two alternatives rests squarely on the shoulders of each Christian.

That third way, "my way," is no different than the second; it is the way of the flesh, too, in that it is not a faith walk. To make matters worse, sometimes even when we think we're walking in the Spirit, we are actually walking after the flesh. This is true simply because our so-called spiritual lives are really being lived in our own strength...on "flesh power."

## Christ as Life

Why did Jesus come *into* you and me instead of along-side, under, behind, or before us? The answer is so important! *Jesus is the only one who has ever lived the victorious Christian life.* He came into you and into me in order to express His life of victory over sin through us. There it is, sweet and simple. That's the new plan, which is as old as the New Testament.

## Sin—More Than Behavior

In order to walk in the Spirit, Scripture instructs us about those things which seek to block us from our goal.

> *Do not go on presenting the members of your body to sin as instruments of righteousness; but present yourselves to God as those alive from the dead, and your members as instruments of righteousness to God* (Romans 6:13).

There are those two "ways" again—I either present myself to God or to something called *sin*. Paul's letter to the Romans, chapters 5 through 8, contains the word "sin" forty-one times. And here's an amazing fact: forty times that word sin is a noun (hamartia; sin); it is a verb only once (hamartano; the act of sinning).

Did you grasp that? "Sin" is a noun in the verse above. But if, as you read it, you interpreted sin as a verb (i.e., stealing hubcaps), then you've missed one of the most powerful truths in the New Testament. There are dozens of verses in the New Testament where sin is a noun (person, place, thing), not a verb (the act of sinning). If you interpret sin in those verses as verbs, your biblical understanding will be comparable to your driving experience when you've taken the wrong exit off the freeway.

In his classic and highly recognized work, *Expository Dictionary of New Testament Words*, W.E. Vine states that in eleven instances after the cross, sin is a "governing power or principle" which is "personified" (p. 1055). *The word "sin" is a power which is represented as a person.* I'm not certain what this word "sin" is in the Bible, but it seems to me that it must be Satan's counterfeit of the Holy Spirit. It is a power which has the ability to wage war against our mind (Romans 7:21-23). Sin has to fight this battle with thoughts or words or images.

In order to clarify this, let's imagine that *sin* is personified as a sergeant, and you are a private under his authority. Now when a sergeant says "frog," a private jumps. He has no choice because a private is under the authority of a sergeant.

The only thing that could break "Sgt. Sin's" hold on you would be either the termination of his authority, or the termination of your obligation to his authority. How could that happen? Through death. If Sgt. Sin should die, you would be free from his authority. If you died, you would certainly be out from under his dictatorial ways. Either way, one of you would have to die in order for you to be set free. With that in mind, now consider this scripture:

> ...*knowing this, that our old self was crucified with Him [you died], that our body of sin might be done away with, that we should no longer be slaves to sin for he who has died is freed from sin* [the noun] (Romans 6:6-7; emphases and brackets added).

Your spiritual death (in Christ) freed you from *sin's* ability to *make* you obey. And now you have, in a sense, been reborn as a civilian, free from the sergeant's authority.

> *...consider yourselves to be dead to sin [the noun], but alive to Christ Jesus* (Romans 6:11).

## Reopened Under New Management

Here's an extremely important part of the gospel that is omitted typically by well-meaning teachers because they have not seen it as reality. You died in Christ when He was crucified (Romans 6:6). Then you were reborn as a new person in Christ at His resurrection (see 2 Corinthians 5:17). The Greek verbs describing this process are all past tense. It's a done deal! This comes with the package when you get saved, and water baptism is a symbolic reenactment of it (Romans 6:4). As a new spirit-being, you are no longer under the authority of Sgt. Sin. You have a *new* Master, Jesus! Your death effected a permanent liberation from sin's tyrannical authority over you. You don't *have* to pay any attention to him now. You are under a new system; thus, you must *act* dead to sin and *alive* to your new Leader, Christ (see Romans 6:13).

Picture the "Sarge" screaming in your ear, demanding that you hit the deck and pick up cigarette butts with your teeth while doing fifty push-ups. Now envision the new you, born anew (not the same old private raised from the dead, by the way!) grinning and saying, "Rain on you, Sarge. You have no more authority over me!"

Dear people, if you know Jesus as your personal Savior and Lord, this is precisely your new relationship to this power the Bible calls "sin" (Romans 6:7).

## Satan's Secret Strategy

Now, let's give sin a couple of aces in the hole. He doesn't give up easily. He knows that your brain was programmed from the years spent under his authority, and although you are a new civilian, you will probably still react in your old military way. (The Bible calls these old ways "flesh" [see Philippians 3:3-9]).

If Sarge could somehow infiltrate your brain and impersonate the old private—you—who used to submit so readily to his authority, then he could constantly "talk" to the *new* you as though you were still under his control! He'd take advantage of your old military conditioning, *use first singular pronouns* (I, me, my, etc.), and "speak" to you with your own accent. You would be deceived into thinking you were reasoning things out in your own mind!

In every situation that you'd encounter, Sgt. Sin would "speak" to you, masquerading as the old private ("old man," "old nature"), intimidating, tempting, accusing, badgering, deceiving you into behaving as if you were still in the service. He'd finally confuse you so much that you'd be convinced you have two personalities, a civilian one (good) and a military one (evil). In fact, this is a common error taught by many well-meaning teachers. If Sgt. Sin were skilled enough, he might even be able to convince you that you had never become a civilian at all. Fortunately, by God's grace, this inner battle has already been won—not by us, but by Christ. Participating in His victory is simply a matter of believing that the indwelling Christ longs to replicate that same victorious life through you. You say, Bill and Anabel, I've never heard this before! Hey, neither had we till God began to reveal it to us after we'd painted ourselves into a corner. He saved our marriage and saved Anabel from probable suicide.

Let me say this: don't swallow biblical teaching from anyone without asking the Holy Spirit to verify it to you through the Bible and by His witness to your own spirit through a sense of inner agreement. We urge you to seek His mind on everything we teach.

Also, the English translation of the Bible which holds more closely to the Hebrew and Greek is the New American Standard version. This is especially true of Romans 5-8. We strongly encourage you to use the NAS translation as you study the truths presented in this book.

## You Will "Life Out" Whatever You Believe About Yourself

For every verse in the New Testament which speaks of Christ indwelling the believer, there are ten verses which state that the believer is in Christ. A ten to one ratio! Scriptures which pertain to your indwelling Christ refer to your death and new birth in Him. Through this death/rebirth process, God changed your spiritual identity from unrighteous to righteous ("all right" with God).

Your essence is spirit. You are a spiritual creature in an earthsuit, not a physical creature with a spirit. God changed your spirit identity by crucifying the old spirit-man/woman and starting all over again, not physically, but spiritually. You are literally a new spirit being!

I strongly suggest that you invest some time researching this very important subject. Look up all the "in Christ" terms in Scripture, including "in Jesus Christ," "in Him," "in Jesus," "in Whom," etc. Take note of the verb tenses and descriptive phrases God uses to speak of you, now that you are a "new creature" in Christ (see 2 Corinthians 5:17). God provided even more than forgiveness for our sins; He changed your spirit identity from sinner man/woman to saint man/woman (holy ones)!

These are God's ways of describing you in His Word. And these descriptions supersede any of the world's personality inventories, the opinions of others, and even your opinion of yourself! Your new birth in Christ gave you a new identity—your true identity now and throughout all eternity.

*Embracing this reality is essential to your victory over sin.*

## You Had to Die Before Being Reborn

Since many Christians do not know that they were crucified in Christ before being reborn, they are doomed to conclude that they are now spiritual schizophrenics. Take a look at some of the biblical evidence that Christians have *literally* died and been reborn as new spirit people:

- Jesus said you can't sew a new patch on an old garment (see Luke 5:36). If you apply this to our identity in Christ, He was saying there is no way you can be a soldier and a civilian simultaneously.
- Jesus said you can't pour new wine into an old skin or it'll rupture (see Mark 2:22). He was saying you can't pour the Holy Spirit into the old soldier. He'd leak! Only civilians can hold Him (see Ezekiel 36:26-27).
- The Word says you can't mix light with darkness (see 2 Corinthians 6:14), yet we've been deceived into believing that we Christians are a bi-polar identity of light and darkness.
- We have been justified (completely forgiven and made righteous) (1 Corinthians 6:11).
- We are at peace with God (Romans 5:1).
- We are accepted (Romans 15:7).
- We are forever free from condemnation (Romans 8:1).
- We are children of God—God is literally our "Papa" (Romans 8:14,15; Galatians 3:26;4:6).
- We are the dwelling places of God, God's new "holy of holies" (1 Corinthians 3:16).
- We are new creations (2 Corinthians 5:17).
- We are the righteousness of God in Christ (2 Corinthians 5:21).
- We are saints (holy ones) (Ephesians 1:1; Philippians 1:1).

- We have direct access to God through the Spirit (Ephesians 2:18).
- We are righteous and holy (Ephesians 4:24).
- We are redeemed and forgiven of all our sins (Colossians 1:14).
- Christ is now our very life (Colossians 3:4).
- We are children of light and not of darkness (1 Thessalonians 5:5).
- We are the enemies of the Deceiver (1 Peter 5:8).
- We are entirely complete in Christ Jesus (Colossians 2:10).

## A House Divided Can Never Stand

Jesus said—in reference to the Deceiver's domain—that "any kingdom [city or house] divided against itself shall not stand" (Matthew 12:25b). So why have we Christians naively believed that each of us has been re-created as a "house divided against him/herself," half civilian and half soldier? I ask you, would God, who "called you out of darkness into His marvelous light" (1 Peter 2:9) deliberately set you up for a "cannot stand" life experience by creating you as a house divided against yourself? No!

Dear Christian, you are not fighting a *civil* war! Those nagging thoughts inside you are not *yours*. It is sin. It is Sgt. Sin impersonating the old man, the old, former you who was crucified with Christ. It is our enemy, Sin. He makes it seem like our old identity is still alive.

There is a tragic difference between contemporary Christianity and that of the first century Christians. Our intimate loved ones and even our high-profile heroes of the faith are falling like flies—God help us! If the heroes can't make it, what chance do the plain vanilla folks in the pew have?

By the grace of God, the ones who can and do make it

are those who discover and appropriate the "mystery... which is Christ in you" (Colossians 1:27). Those of us who not only survive, but who are "more than conquerors through Him" have discovered that *we cannot live the Christian life,* but that the One who lives within us *can.* We have accepted our true identity in Christ, and how we can let Him live through us to overcome the power of sin. (A thorough treatment of the truth of our identity in Christ and its practical application is available in *Lifetime Guarantee,* by Bill Gillham [Eugene, Oregon; Harvest House Publishers, 1993].)

## Making Christian Marriages Work

So what does all this have to do with marital discord? How does it apply to discouraged wives, disappointed husbands and disillusioned couples? How can it heal the heartbreak faced by disintegrating families? How does this marriage book hold any more hope for us than others? In the pages that follow, you will discover how the reality of Christ's-life-in-you will enable you and your spouse to make your marriage work. You'll also see how, without that reality, we very nearly destroyed our own relationship as well as each other. You'll hear from each of us how we've been changed from the inside out by the life of Christ.

## Grace Upon Grace

*He Said, She Said* is more than a catchy title. It is our way of giving different perspectives within the same book. You'll read some words from Anabel, others from Bill, and still others from both of us. We hope you'll read the book together—perhaps you'll even want to read it aloud. We pray that by sharing our personal story, you'll see how Christ is living His agape-love through us and how He will do the same for you!

*Christ in me, the hope of glory. Hope*—what a beautiful word. In our roles as husbands and wives, in everything we do as Christians, it's imperative that we come to understand this powerful truth of Christ in and through us and apply Him to all aspects of our lives. He is our only hope for walking in victory through the dark and dangerous days we face.

# FLESH VS. FLESH = DISASTER

*God has certain laws which He has
designed for us as husband and wife.
These laws, like gravity, are designed
for our good, and if we violate them,
something is going to go splat.*

# Chapter Two

Anabel: The buffet. The pie safe. The round oak table. The "piano desk." Those old pieces of furntiture weren't antiques when we bought them—they were the cheapest things we could find at the secondhand furniture store. Now that we've grown older, the furniture has become more valuable. (People seem to be about the only things that don't become more valuable with age!)

Punched tin cabinet doors. Vintage milk bottles. A time-worn cracker keeper. A soda-straw dispenser. As we look around at these simple things sitting on the shelves, we feel mixed emotions—emotions that have been carefully deposited in our "memory banks" throughout the years we have been husband and wife.

## Dreams vs. Reality

As a young bride, I entered into the holy realm of marriage with such high expectations. Of course I had high expectations for every area in my life, but I so wanted my marriage to be "perfect."

Bill and I were part of the generation of "love songs..."

> *Every time we say good-bye, I die a little*
> *One love will satisfy as long as I live*
> *My devotion is endless and deep as the ocean*
> *This isn't sometimes, this is always*
> *Try a little tenderness*
> *He's just my Bill*

...but somehow the love songs just weren't coming true. Our marriage wasn't as "perfect" as I wanted it to be. Life wasn't working out the way I had planned.

## Dreams of Personal Satisfaction

**Bill:** When Anabel recalls the expectations she had as we entered into marriage, I am always painfully aware of just how immature I was, and how unprepared I was for stepping through such a life-changing door into the future.

I may as well be honest. As a virgin, my highest priority for marriage was to have this beautiful woman satisfy my physical needs. At the time, that was my definition of heaven, since it seemed to be the primary thing missing from my life. I had a good job, a promising future, and good friends to hunt and fish with. I figured that if I could just get the marriage business behind me so my burning passion would be satisfied, it would cease to interfere with my other recreational interests. Life would then be smooth sailing.

As for those love songs Anabel cited? Sure, they were special; but when I heard them, they were simply an overture to the bedroom. My concern was to get *my* needs satisfied—period. I was consumed with me, myself and I.

And as the flesh would have it, when the smoke cleared from the honeymoon and we settled into married life, other appetites began to escalate: I wanted a new car, a new house, a boat and motor for fishing. And I wanted to keep climbing the career ladder.

Other matters caused further complications. Once the marriage bed had removed some of my inhibition about being more sexually aggressive, I began a more serious analysis of the fences surrounding life's "greener pastures." I was in a deep hole full of needs, and at the bottom of it all, I was a frustrated, unhappy man.

**Anabel:** Bill and I were both hurting. Let me review a typical scene from the first few years of our blissful married life. Mother and Dad were coming for a visit, so I wanted the house to be perfect. I needed to have rods put up for new curtains. However, asking Bill to do things like that never seemed to turn out all that well (to put it mildly!). I finally gathered my courage and broached the subject.

Yes, Bill condescended to put up the curtain rods, but his every word and movement indicated that this certainly was *not* something he enjoyed doing. I knew what was going on in his mind: *No woman tells me what to do. Why does she have to put up silly curtains anyway? Dumb woman. She's always trying to control my time.*

Meanwhile, my thoughts reflected my own anxiety. *Oh, Lord, don't let him hit his finger. Don't let him bend the nail! Please don't let anything go wrong.*

I was very conscious of my every move. I wanted to be sure to hand him the hammer with the handle rotated in the "right" direction, but I'd forgotten which direction was the right direction!

"Could you please hand that hammer to me the right way?"

"I'm sorry."

"Well, I've told you how to do it ten times. I don't see why you want me to work on these dumb curtains, anyway. The windows looked okay the way they were!"

By now there was a lump in my throat, and my emotions were threatening to spill out all over the place—not exactly what I had in mind for my folks' visit!

## God's Way—Making Things Work

**Bill:** Now, why in the world would I be acting like such a hammerhead? And why would Anabel be so insecure and scared in our relationship? To answer those questions, we'd like you to meet Mr. Threatened Macho Flesh and Mrs. Super Sensitivity Flesh—Bill and Anabel. We want to describe our "flesh patterns" to you and show how allowing those patterns to control us nearly destroyed our marriage.

First of all, we must understand that God has established certain laws on earth. Take the law of gravity for example. It's for our good—it keeps us from falling off the planet, makes water slides work, and so forth. But if you violate it, you'll go splat.

God also has certain laws which He has designed for us as husband and wife, and He is not an arbitrary Person. Marriage laws, like gravity, are designed for our good, and if we violate them, something is going to go *splat*. It may be us, the marriage, or the kids, but something is going to suffer until we get our "ducks lined up" according to what He says.

The job description of a god is, "He runs things." There is only one true God, and if we are ever to experience His peace, we must let Him rule us. He will never let us "enter into His rest" as long as we're making up our own rules.

## Lord of the Ring

Let me use myself as an example. I'll begin with my childhood, so you can see how my fleshly pattern of behavior was developed.

Mom and Pop made some mistakes, but I cannot blame my folks for my hang-ups. I generated those hang-ups striving to get my needs met in their home. I love them, and I wouldn't change my past because I am now able to see it as being a part of my pilgrimage with Christ.

God is Love, so God created each of us with a basic human need to be loved, because if we didn't need love, we wouldn't need God. Neat idea, huh?

But, when you and I showed up on Planet Earth we knew nothing of God, so we set out to satisfy our need for love. Each of us drew an imaginary circle around ourselves and declared ourselves god (ruler) of our circle. Then we made up our own rules, striving to get our needs met. I call this *"playing Lord of the Ring."* And this *"Lord of the Ring"* action is another way of describing original sin.

A baby is a totally self-centered little "lord of the ring." If he awakens at 2:00 a.m. cold, wet, and hungry, he doesn't lie there and think, *Poor Mom. I just can't make her get up again tonight. She needs her rest. I'll tough it out until daylight.*

No way! The baby says, "Hey! Wake up! Come fix the kid!"

## I Did It My Way

Because of this self-centeredness, the baby learns about no one but himself from the feedback he gets from others. He learns nothing about the people around him.

For example, if his folks don't kiss him, he doesn't conclude that it's difficult for them to show affection. He simply learns, *I'm unkissable. Who'd want to kiss me?*

Through self-centered reasoning, the child choreographs fleshly patterns for living in his family—his "ring."

Now, it's important to understand that our emotions "knee-jerk" to our minds. If you set your mind on a fearful stimulus, like a snarling Doberman pinscher, you'll *feel* fearful. If you set your mind that you're unkissable, you'll *feel* unkissable. If you set your mind there consistently, on a one-to-ten scale, your "feeler" will become stuck on an eight. By the time you are five years old, all the points beneath the eight will erode away.

If your feeler tells you you're an "eight" on unkissability most of the time, you'll eventually believe in your mind that it's true. A flesh pattern has been programmed into your brain.

## A Male Ego Trip?

Now back to me and how my specific fleshly patterns developed. As a little boy, it was imperative that I learn to accept myself as male. How could I accomplish this? At age six I needed to feel that I could kick a ball better than a girl, that I could sweat more than she could, or that I could handle snakes. In short, I needed to *feel* that I was the stronger of the genders. God made me that way. It wasn't an ego trip; it was simply a matter of being male. It's as normal for boys to be that way as it is for girls to want to wear their mothers' high-heeled shoes. We're designed to be dragon slayers.

My Mom and Pop were lords of the ring, too. They had established their marriage contrary to God's plan, in that Mom actually "lifed out"—acted out in her daily life—the role of husband, and Pop "lifed out" the role of wife. This was an upside down arrangement, according to

God's ways. Pop totally submitted to Mom's authority over him. He was a very passive man. If I ever asked his permission to do anything, he'd say, "Go ask your mom." I finally rejected him as my male role model and quit asking him.

Mom passed the physical for being a female, and therefore represented womanhood to me. As I learned to accept myself as a male, I had to see myself as progressively becoming stronger than Mom. That was something like climbing Mt. Everest! Nobody was stronger than my mother. We described her as being "strong as an acre of garlic"—behind her back.

Some sons are so intimidated in a setting like this that, with a lot of help from the Deceiver, they do a 180 turn and become homosexual. Others semi-surrender their masculinity by aping their father's role model and become passive. This is what my dad had done as a kid. These males go through life submitting to everyone, hoping to gain acceptance by never rocking the boat. Still others rebel at their mom's dominance over them and fight back; they disdain their dad's passivity and reject him as a role model. They set out to prove their masculinity to *themselves*, and they develop macho flesh patterns.

I chose option three. As I played lord of my ring, I was striving to be masculine. How could I prove my masculinity to myself? I could become vulgar and profane. I could become an athlete, earn a letterman's jacket, work at developing a "don't-tread-on-me" look in my eyes, and attempt to be a mean machine. Unfortunately, this was pretty difficult because as a late bloomer my earthsuit at age fifteen was 5'2" and weighed 110 pounds. When I finally bloomed and became a football starter I knew there really was a God.

What else could I do? I could seduce the high school

girls. That's macho. The problem was that no one ever kissed anybody in our family. Mom didn't even let the dog lick us. So I *felt* unkissable. My feeler was stuck. I didn't get into sex. Hey, I had to struggle to get into kissing! All my sexual encounters took place in my thought-life—a flesh pattern, by the way, that would eventually plague me in my adult life as a Christian.

All these elements were involved in the development of my flesh patterns.

## My Archenemies

One particular group of people evolved into my arch enemies. They were a constant reminder to me of my weakness, and of my inability to accept myself as a "real" male. Who were they? Strong, outspoken, assertive women. They threatened my masculinity just as Mom had. I spewed my internal frustration onto them in the form of insults, sarcasm, criticism, and ridicule. Strong women blocked me from accepting myself. They messed up my ring.

Then I got married. What sort of a woman did I marry? One who would relieve the pressure, right? Wrong. I married one who was strong as an acre of garlic. You ask, "Well, why did you do that?"

Because my feeler was stuck! I *felt* like a boy trying to enter a man's world with a man's responsibilities, and I couldn't hack it. So I married someone who could carry the load of both roles in the relationship. Then when she did so well, it ate my lunch! So after the honeymoon was over, I began to unleash my never-ending supply of criticism, sarcasm, and hostility against females onto my precious wife.

I tried to destroy Anabel.

## Transformed by a Renewed Mind

After I came to Christ at age twenty-nine, all my old patterns for living became the equivalent of my "old ways," my unique version of the "flesh," similar to what Paul describes in Philippians 3:4-7. I had become a "new creature," and my behavior changed in many ways.

However, even though I was saved, the old hostility and criticism of Anabel actually seemed to get worse. I had programmed my brain badly all my life, and I was still walking after the flesh. In the public eye, I was a personal soul winner. But I was a destroyer in my own home. And I couldn't quit.

Finally, after thirteen years of frustration, trying and failing to live the Christian life, God brought me to the end of *my* resources. He showed me, through my weakness, that He hadn't put Christ inside me to help me, but to express *His Life through me.* I failed in my own ability to carry myself through the deepest crises in my life. This failure proved to be the key to discovering Christ *as* my Life.

## An Award–Winning Performance

**Anabel:** During those traumatic years of our marriage, an outside observer would have looked at me and said, "She doesn't have any problems." But to me, life was a bottomless pit with oil-slick walls and quicksand on the bottom. My feverish flailing only caused me to sink further. I couldn't bail myself out of the awful hole I was in. I was unhappy. Frustrated. Hurting. Barely surviving.

I went into marriage with some very positive attributes. I was an efficient, outgoing, self-confident person with an impressive record: junior high student council representative, senior high student council president, drum major, valedictorian, voted most popular girl on campus in college—I was "performing" well. My whole life had been built around performance-based acceptance, and when you live with that pattern for years, you generally evolve toward performance-based self-acceptance.

To make matters worse, somewhere along the line I began thinking: *If you accept me when I perform well, what would you do if I performed perfectly?* With that idea, another yoke of bondage, self-condemnation and constant introspection was draped around my neck! Add to that an emotional web of being supersensitive to any kind of critical evaluation—and that web caught the slightest movement toward criticism. *"Don't tell me I did it wrong! I did not do it wrong—I did it perfectly—I stayed up past midnight to be sure and certain that it was done to perfection!"*

## The Poison of Perfectionism

In the final analysis I was the one that my performance had to please—perfectly. What a mess, and what a fragile technique for acceptance from others as well as from myself.

Bill was a perfectionist, too—only he didn't demand perfect performance out of himself. He demanded it out of the people around him, the people who were supposed to meet his needs. This is one of the characteristics of a person with "indulged flesh" patterns. These two patterns—being a super performer/perfectionist and being supersensitive about critical remarks—nearly destroyed me, my marriage, and my family.

My techniques for getting acceptance and love in the years before marriage had been very successful. A performer is driven to achieve, and though I was discouraged when I didn't do well, there was always another tomorrow, another chance, another contest. But this was it! The big event—marriage—had arrived, and I wasn't winning. Instead, I was being torn apart. To top it all, I couldn't get out of this "contest" and enter another one.

During my years in school, I learned to protect my "perfect" image by never having any close friends; I didn't want anyone to see me when I was not "up" and performing well. You see, my mind-set was that people would not accept or like me if I did not perform well enough to please them. Sadly, my marriage had validated this way of thinking. Bill knew me. Bill didn't like me. My fears were justified. You get to know me, and you won't like me. My techniques weren't working anymore, and my self-esteem began to plummet.

## The Truth About "Mr. Wonderful"

I hadn't prayed about the person I was to marry. Bill and I dated steadily for five years. We were constant companions. Surely you know someone after being constant companions for five years, don't you? I thought I knew Bill. He was very considerate, and kind. He never cursed or told off-color stories. He was simply "Mr. Wonderful." Then we got married, and when he got me into the castle with the drawbridge up, this tender, pure, generous, thoughtful, kind young man changed incredibly.

The most horrible change involved the things he said to me. One Saturday morning in our first little honeymoon apartment, Bill said, "Honey, I'd like to talk to you for a moment." He took me by the hand and led me into our living room. We sat down on the little flowered settee (which I had just re-covered—and it looked very nice, thank you), and he said, very gently, "Honey, I wish that you would learn to do at least one thing well."

**Bill:** What a guy…

**Anabel:** I thought I was doing pretty well, but obviously I wasn't. Perhaps Bill expected his words to destroy me—remember his game plan was to destroy strong, capable women. But his expectations were wrong. His criticism motivated me to do bigger, better and more perfect things. You see, the lifeblood of a performer is praise, and I was trying to get Bill to praise me. If you don't get the praise you need, you begin to die. So I was engaged in a life-and-death battle—and I was losing. Oh, but I was going to fight.

## The Battle for Praise

When Bill moonlighted in the oil fields during his summer break from teaching, he would leave the house at 7:30 in the morning and get home at 5:00, dirty, tired, hungry, and in a bad mood. My thinking was: *What can I do for Bill today to please him? I know! I'll mow and edge the lawn, prune the hedges, and rake everything up. Then, when he comes home, he'll say, "Would you look at this lawn. Talk about manicured! Did you do all of this by yourself? How great it looks!" Surely he will notice and praise me!*

No, he didn't.

Good performer that I am, I didn't give up. By now I was starving for praise, so I would try harder the next day. Another idea: *I'll have a freezer of his favorite ice cream sitting on the porch, and when he sees it, he'll say, "What a wife you are! I can't think of anything that would please me more than a dish of ice cream right now!" He'll say something like that, won't he...please?*

But he didn't.

Another tomorrow—another "try" day. My new plan: *I'll start saving pennies from our very meager budget and buy some steaks. Then, when Bill sits down to the supper table, he will say, "What a marvel you are with this budget.*

*To think that you could save enough money to have a supper like this. I am so proud of you!" He will say that, won't he?*

No, he wouldn't.

**Bill:** As Anabel and I look back on this horror story and analyze it, we can see what was happening to us. I was very insecure in my masculinity and was trying to stamp out every evidence or "proof" that Anabel was capable and independent—one of those "strong" women that threatened me so much.

Anabel was striving to perform, twice as well as anyone should be expected to perform, in order to get praise from me and to preserve her self-esteem.

We were the immovable object meeting the indestructible force, and we eventually crashed in flames.

**Anabel:** Bill couldn't destroy me by criticizing my performance. I was too strong for that, so he eventually switched plans. He began pointing out things that I couldn't change. For instance, one time we were going to a square dance and I, of course, looked perfect. (Performers always look perfect. They don't leave the house until they do!). Bill looked over at me in my frilly square-dance dress and said, "You know, I really can't imagine anyone wanting to dance with you." It would be an understatement to say that I didn't enjoy the square dance.

If we were walking out the door for an evening of fun, Bill would casually remark, "Try not to laugh so much this evening. You really make people uncomfortable when you do that." Before long, these new tactics began to work. Bill's game plan for destroying me was showing signs of success.

After seven years of marriage, Bill became a Christian. He began to realize what he had become and he called out to God. God heard him and knew the depths of his desire, the sincerity of his heart, and responded to his cry of repentance. Through the miracle of the new birth, that man is no more. However, his behavior was not an "overnight" miracle—his horrible sarcastic tongue remained.

## "I Give Up! I Can't Do It!"

Let's look down the road—twenty years into the marriage. I had not given up, but by then I had developed a coping mechanism for existing: depression, deep depression. In that state of mind, you can't remember anything nice happening yesterday, and you have no hope that something nice will happen tomorrow. You just have today, and I had learned from the man I lived with that I did not perform well on "todays." I wanted out and the only acceptable out for a performer is suicide—that way you don't have to face people after your poor performance. This was my state of mind when the Lord spoke to me.

Oh, I wanted our marriage to work so badly. I had read and reread Ephesians 5:33b from the Amplified Bible about respecting and loving and honoring your husband. I couldn't do all of those things. I didn't even want to be around Bill. I didn't like him.

I had gone to bed. It had been a bad day, but I don't remember why, because I had a lot of bad days. I was sobbing and talking to the Lord: "God, I don't understand what is going on in my life. My marriage is so far from what I long for it to be and what I know You intended it to be. My kids are not turning out the way I want them to, and Lord, I am so tired. I'm weary. I've given and given and given, and I just don't think that I can give anymore."

Then I said something that I had never said in all of my forty some-odd years, something that is very difficult for any performer to say: "Lord, I give up. *I can't do it!*

"If anything is going to come of this marriage, if anything is going to come out of these kids, You're going to have to do it; I can't."

God spoke to me that night. Thoughts came to mind that were foreign to my way of thinking, and by faith I believe those thoughts were a message from the Lord. It was a simple little phrase: "Thank you, Anabel. I'll do it all for you." That was the beginning, and I do mean the *beginning*. Step by step by sometimes painful step, I have learned and am learning the truth of Galatians 2:20:

> *I have been crucified with Christ; and it is no longer I who live, but Christ lives in me; and the life which I now live in the flesh [as the wife of Bill Gillham, as the mother of Pres, Mace, Will, and Wade, whether I am teaching, making a banana cream pie, digging in the marigolds or cleaning the commode] I live by faith in the Son of God, who loved me, and delivered Himself up for me.*

What an incredible difference that truth has made in my life!

**Bill:** Those were hard times. They were hard for both of us, and I plead guilty to wearing the "black hat." I ought to have been shot. I was destroying Anabel with my critical tongue, just as she was destroying me with her strength. We were mutually destroying each other. We did not understand how to let Christ live through us in order to straighten out the mess we had created.

Things were about to change, but we had a lot to learn.

# IS MARRIAGE FOR REAL?

———— ✦ ————

*"Let marriage be held in
honor among all"
(Hebrews 13:4).*

———— ✦ ————

# Chapter Three

**B**ill: The changes that transformed our marriage didn't happen overnight. As you continue to read, you'll find more stories about the Gillhams, as well as other couples we've counseled. We hope that some of our hard-learned lessons will help you see strengths and weaknesses in your own relationship.

## Is Our Culture Marriage-Friendly?

A primary contributor to the high divorce rate in our country is the popular culture that surrounds us. And it is one big reason that the two of us came into our honeymoon destined for trouble. I had been heavily influenced by the environment I grew up in. My view of women reflected the John Wayne role model I wanted to identify with. Anabel mirrored her cultural background, too. She was a top achiever, a gifted performer, and she fit easily into a world that increasingly encourages competitiveness, power and independence in wives. Besides all that, our idea of marriage itself was off-base. It was pieced together from our childhood families, from films and from fantasies we had developed. As we go along, we'll use our marital journey to illustrate our points and suggestions. You're looking for answers, we want to help you find them every way we can.

Many people in today's world have warped views of marriage, and God's biblical model is generally considered archaic. We have stored it away in the attic in a box marked "Don't throw away—may come back in style." But the fact is, it will never become obsolete. This beautiful excerpt of a conversation between an older man and his younger male colleague captures a glimpse of a godly marriage, and how it is supposed to work.

> *"Your wife must love you very much."*
> *"Of course! She is my wife."*
> *"It does not necessarily follow that she must love you. Many wives stop loving their husbands."*
> *"Ah, that shows how little you truly understand marriage. No wife ever stopped loving her husband, when he was truly loving her as a man was intended to love a woman."*
> *"Are you saying people do not fall in love, and then out of it again?"*
> *"What has falling in love to do with marriage? Nothing! You are not married, are you?"*
> *"Actually, I am married."*
> *"Then for your sake—and your wife's—I hope*

*that someday soon you leave behind this foolishness about being 'in love.' No marriage can survive unless it gets past that and to the love of sacrifice. Ah, but you are young!"*

*"But you said your wife loved you. I assume you love her?"*

*"Of course! Of course! We are in love now because we first learned how to sacrifice ourselves one to the other. We have learned to serve, to lay down our lives, to wash each other's feet, so to speak. You don't do those kinds of things year after year unless you are determined to love. Not in love, but determined to love."*

*"I guess I always thought love had to come first in a marriage."*

*"No, my friend. Love—that comes second! First comes commitment, sacrifice. Then, and only then, comes true and lasting love. That is why my wife and I are now in love."*

[Adapted with permission from Michael Phillips and Judith Pella, *Shadows Over Stonewycke* (Minneapolis: Bethany House Publishers, 1988).]

**Anabel:** That's so far from our culture's present perspective of marriage, isn't it? Today's views come in a wide assortment of variations.

## Fantasy Marriages

First, there is the fantasy approach. Our kids are constantly bombarded with such relationships through movies, music and television. The media would have us believe that love is one great romantic fling—passion that never seems to wane—and if it does, you simply move on to another relationship.

It is so difficult to convince two kids with stars in their eyes that Prince Charming and Sleeping Beauty exist only in fairy tales, and that the absolute bottom line of marriage is spelled C-O-M-M-I-T-M-E-N-T. You have to work at it. As the reading above so eloquently indicates, love does not hold the marriage together. It is marriage that holds the love together.

## Casual Vows

Then there is the casual approach. Even as the groom is standing at the altar watching this vision of loveliness float down the aisle, both he and the bride may have in the back of their minds this thought: "If it doesn't work out, we can always get a divorce."

Divorce is socially acceptable these days—there's no stigma attached to it anymore, which makes it almost easy to say, "I'm unhappy with you. I didn't know it was going to be this way. I don't want to live with you anymore." Every time those words are said, another divorce statistic rings up.

## Cultural Taboos vs. the Holy Spirit's Restraint

**Bill:** God is doing a new work in our day. He is allowing the Devil to declare "open season" on all cultural taboos against sin while increasingly revealing Himself and His availability to us, through us, to overcome sin.

Thirty years ago in small town, USA, if a man abandoned his wife and married his secretary, the townspeople would ostracize him along with his new wife. If they wanted to avoid the pain they'd have to move away and start anew. You see, the Holy Spirit was not restraining marriages from going to the divorce court. A cultural taboo against sin...fear of community rejection was the false restrainer. Not today! Even some preachers who have pulled such shenanigans are welcomed with open arms to continue pastoring. No repentance, no discipline.

I believe this is but the beginning; that God is going to let it get so hot in the kitchen that no believer who walks in flesh-power will be able to live an overcoming life. Our wonderful, jealous, Heavenly Father is allowing all Christians to be painted into a corner to crowd us toward discovering Christ as Life that He might overcome sin *for* us.

## Living Separate Lives

**Anabel:** I suppose that the warped view of marriage we see most frequently is that of "building separate lives." If the wife could verbalize her thoughts, she might say: "I really don't mind, husband, that you jet all over the country, that you are in London one week and Lisbon the next."

Or, "It doesn't really bother me that your territory now covers four states instead of three and that you're gone the majority of the time."

Or, "I don't care if you play softball three nights a week and go fishing every weekend. That's okay with me."

"You see, husband, I get along better without you than I do with you. I don't need you. I've given up on you. I've built my own life. I have Bible Study Fellowship Leader's Meeting on Monday, bridge club on Tuesdays, Bible Study Fellowship every Wednesday, volunteer hospital duty every Thursday. I jog on Monday, Wednesday and Friday, and attend a museum and fine arts committee meeting monthly. I really don't need you anymore."

And if she's a working wife, she may send a different message: "My career is very satisfying to me. I find great pleasure in it, and I believe I'm making a difference in my world. My life is very fulfilled—without you in it."

**Bill:** It breaks my heart to see these couples who once

had stars in their eyes and sweet promises on their lips, letting their marriages seep through the cracks because they've built separate lives. God never intended that for marriage; He said "the two shall become one."

When we describe these views in our seminars, some couples don't seem to get it. They laugh and say, "Oh, we wave to each other as we meet in the driveway, but that's about it."

**Anabel:** Someone has said it this way: "Our marriage is held together by thin strands of thread called 'the children,' or 'our financial status,' or 'our reputation in the community.'" They know nothing of the beautiful oneness God intended for us to experience in our marriages. The following letter reveals how the heartbreak grows.

> *Dear Anabel,*
> *With John and me there was nothing. We compromised and worked our way through a million crises, but after at least ten years of just sharing the same house, where even idle conversation ended in raw nerves, what can we do but call it quits?*
> *I sat down and wrote "What Went Wrong Along the Way," at the top of a piece of typing paper the day before the divorce was final. I wrote for three and one-half hours before I quit. It was a gradual twenty-year process. Oh, we were very happy when my whole world revolved around him and his work.*
> *I think this has had a lot to do with our growing apart. It was a very subtle, deep-down, hairline crack in the dike that simply grew and grew. He pulled within himself and built a wall that was rarely opened to me. I shrugged it off and went out into my world of music and church-caring people and in the quiet times felt lonely.*

*That, of course, was only part of the problem, but it was a major part. Togetherness is so important, as you well know, and John and I never did anything together. Most people didn't even know I had a husband because I was always alone. And he was always alone when he went somewhere—which was seldom. So we were two lonely people who just lived together.*

**Bill:** Considering all the heartache we've seen, it doesn't surprise us that young people live together outside the marriage vows. The reasoning is simply this: "If living with someone for six or eight months will keep me from getting into the hell that my parents glibly called marriage, then I'll try it with no strings attached." Unfortunately, statistics tell us that living together first doesn't guarantee a happy ending—couples who live together before marrying actually have a higher divorce rate than those who don't.

## The Female Nonentity

**Anabel:** Then there is the view of marriage that was espoused from pulpits not too many years ago and is still held tenaciously by some. It glorifies a very gifted, grand and noble male who puts up with—indeed, endures—a little timid, mealy-mouthed, mousy nonentity called the female, who never has a worthwhile thought in her head. "Nonentity" means a person or thing of little or no importance.

**Bill:** Years ago our pastor cited a particular couple in our fellowship as the epitome of what a Christian marriage ought to be; we were exhorted to emulate their example. We'll call this couple John and Mary. We had been in their home that very week to see how their redecorating was progressing.

"What color are you going to paint your kitchen, Mary?" I asked.

"I don't know. John hasn't told me yet," Mary responded.

That was fairly typical of their interaction. You got the idea that when John was hungry he'd snap his fingers, say, "kitchen," and she'd fire out to build him a sandwich. At times, I guess he'd snap his fingers and say, "bedroom," too. Mary operated at about the same level as a good cocker spaniel.

Folks, as we understand the Bible, that example of passivity is not what God has in mind for a wife. That dear wife would have interacted with her husband in that same manner if she had never met Jesus. That's not Christian submission; it's "chicken flesh." She operated out of a fear of men. (Incidentally, we're happy to report that John and Mary have turned things around now. They made the necessary change by gaining a new understanding of how to appropriate Christ as Life through them.)

**Anabel:** But how does a woman become as passive as Mary was? Was she born that way? No, she developed that passivity herself. As a child she learned that by submitting to all power figures, both male and female, she could gain their acceptance and love. The more she submitted, the less friction she experienced; and for her, less friction meant greater love and acceptance.

**Bill:** Her goal was to "never make waves." If she ever stated an opinion and sensed it was rejected by another person, she took it personally, believing he or she was rejecting her. Since that felt very unpleasant, she developed the practice of never expressing an opinion. Finally she arrived at the point where she didn't even know what her opinion was a great deal of the time. As we'd say back home, "She became anybody's dog that would hunt with her."

Consider this question: is this woman "lifing out" her new identity in Christ, or is she manifesting her unique version of the flesh? She's being controlled by her old ways, her "flesh" (ref. Philippians 3:4-7 again). God does not give birth to *passive* new men or women in Christ. That passivity is a do-it-yourself project. True biblical submission differs from passivity. But many Christian women—and their husbands—misunderstand that.

## An "Unpardonable Sin"?

A woman in her forties came up to me after we had spoken at a couples retreat in Florida. She was tentative in her manner, glancing around as she tearfully related how she had always been a "submissive wife," but that her husband, a godly man whom she dearly loved, had a terrible temper. She assured me that she had never mentioned this to "any living soul," then went on to say that when he lost his temper and yelled at her, it just crushed her. Her custom, after Sam's angry explosions, was to go quietly to her bedroom, close the door and cry, never letting him see her reaction.

She said she had committed what seemed an unpardonable sin three months before when, following one of his tirades, she confronted him by saying, "Sam, I just can't handle your temper any longer! I don't think I can keep going like this. I feel like it's eventually going to kill me. I'm having severe headaches."

"Then I just fell apart crying," she said. "I've always been such a submissive wife. I just don't know how I could have done such a terrible thing." She wept quietly into her handkerchief.

"What did Sam say when you confronted him like that?"

"He took me in his arms and held me and said he was

so sorry he had been hurting me all these years and that he wouldn't hurt me for the world. He hasn't lost his temper since! But, I just feel so bad for having done that; I've always been a submissive wife and I know I've failed the Lord. I just don't know what made me do such a thing."

"How did Sam feel about your confronting him with his temper problem?"

"Oh, he has grieved over his behavior."

"Sweet Sister, agape love means 'I will do the most redemptive, edifying, constructive thing I can think of for you.' I believe you were under the control of the Holy Spirit when you confronted Sam. God had to let you come to that point of such utter despair, frustration, and even anger so that you would be motivated to confront your husband. He's been wanting to do this through you for years, and now, because of the change in Sam's behavior, He has given you hard evidence that He was at work through you.

"Now you are letting sin accuse you when in fact you ministered agape to your husband. You are believing that this internal condemnation is the Holy Spirit convicting you. No! That's false guilt from Satan. You didn't rebel; you loved Sam. It was a courageous thing you did for him. All these years you have been operating from your stuck feeler on a 'fear-of-man' basis. Because of your fear of rejection, your lord-of-the-ring technique has been to never make waves. Much of your passive submission was not Christ. Instead, it was based on a fear that you'd lose your husband's love by making him upset with you. That's your flesh."

## Trivial Pursuit or High Calling?

**Anabel:** Besides experiencing unkindness, another common complaint from wives is that husbands sometimes make them feel like nonentities by implying that the work they do around the house is unimportant. We once saw a cartoon, depicting a husband who said, "You stick to your washing, ironing, cooking and scrubbing. No wife of mine is going to work!" This pretty well sums up the perspective of some males—housekeeping is labeled a "trivial pursuit."

And society plays right into this attitude. The world-system propaganda that inundates us goes something like this: "You really should place your child in a day-care center. It will enhance his social adjustment, and he will then quickly acclimate to elementary school."

Wow! There goes the mothering role that many women believed was so very important. How important was it? So much so that a woman would actually keep her little one out of school an extra year so she could instill in him her standards, her moral values, and her deep convictions. That's been taken away, because mothering doesn't really seem all that important anymore.

Then there is the subtle suggestion that men's sex lives would be enhanced if they could enjoy sort of a "sexual smorgasbord" with several partners. Just any woman can give sexual satisfaction—sometimes much more effectively than a wife with Victorian standards. And there goes that very intimate relationship that wives thought was theirs alone. It was to be a very special relationship that only I would have, and as my husband and I would look at each other across a crowded room, there would be a secret message in our eyes—he would know me as no other man would. That's gone. It isn't important anymore.

And, of course, advertisers send me the message that having the right bottle under the sink means that just any clod can keep house, step out the door in record breaking time, and, looking back at a shiny floor, find *true* fulfillment in the real working world.

*I am not a housekeeper; I am a homemaker.* There is an incredible difference. The job classification does not revolve around "trivia."

## The Career of a Lifetime

You know, when there are a lot of ladies together and they're asked to introduce themselves and tell what they do, those who don't work outside the home feel pressured to call themselves something clever like "domestic engineers" or "household maintenance experts." Is there something wrong with saying "We are wives. We are mothers"?

It's terribly important for children to smell cookies baking when they come home from school. It's important for my husband to smell supper cooking (even if it's just an onion in the oven). Mothers are training their boys in "what-I-want-in-a-wife"; they are teaching their daughters how to function in the role of wife and mother. Mothers are building a refuge, a haven, a place of security wrapped in and governed by love.

Wives are creating a place where their husbands do not have to compete, where order prevails, and where pressures are alleviated as much as possible. These are important concerns. They are vital to the welfare of every family.

But, in today's culture, all of that has been taken away from women. Females have come out fighting, fists clenched, saying, "I am somebody, and I will prove it to you, man! I will do whatever you do as well as you—or better! I am not a nonentity!"

## Career Women

**Bill:** Too many of us try to make our marriages work in our own strength, when most of all, we need to understand our God-ordained roles. But does that mean that a wife and mom can never be in God's will if she's gainfully employed?

**Anabel:** That's a question we're often asked by women. Many will cite the "Proverbs 31 Woman" as a scriptural role model of a wife who was a very successful business-woman. However, as you read about this enterprising woman's lifestyle, and try to see her as your wife/career woman role model, be sure to place a retinue of servants in her home and understand that her husband "sits in the gate." This means he's a community leader and is very successful. He is not passive, nor is he a threatened male. That makes an incredible difference.

Some women *have* to work. They are the sole bread-winners in fragmented families. Others have to work because of certain circumstances in their lives. They have no choice. We understand that. But the Bible clarifies the role of the woman who has a choice.

## The Revealed Will vs. the Impressed Will of God

**Bill:** Have you ever realized the difference between the revealed will of God and the impressed will of God?

The *revealed* will of God is the direct Word of God...the Bible. There are no questions about it. When God's will is revealed, I don't wait to "feel" anything; I don't put out a fleece; I don't ask Him thirty-six times if He is sure. I simply read it and then heed it. "You shall love your neighbor as yourself," for example, doesn't leave anything to the imagination.

The revealed will of God is direct instruction—instruction that I am to place as my highest priority.

The *impressed* will of God is different. It isn't high-lighted or underlined in my Bible. I can't find it in the concordance. I just "believe" the Holy Spirit is leading and since this impression is not countermanded in the Bible, it is what I am to do. Who you marry, the job you take, how much your offering should be for the visiting speaker, where you should go to school—these all fall under the category of the "impressed will of God."

## Always Leave the Wrong Impression

**Anabel:** Here's a story that illustrates the difference. Suppose both you and your husband are very dedicated Christians. He's a pastor, and you've recently moved to a different town to take over the leadership of a new church. Together, you feel impressed that this church is the one God wants him to shepherd.

You're both walking in the impressed will of God.

But your husband is having to devote a great deal more time to this new church than he had initially expected. It's a larger church than the one you had before, and people pull at him from every direction. Committee meetings swallow up two nights a week; there's lunch nearly every day with one of the church leaders; his counseling load has escalated until he feels as if he has the whole world on his shoulders. Meanwhile...

You are neglected.

The children are neglected.

The "nest" is neglected.

He is so stressed out that the times when he *is* at home are tension-filled. Although he believes he is operating under the impressed will of God, he is violating the revealed will of God.

Now, let's just suppose that you, as that man's wife, tell people, "I try not to bother my husband with household details or with problems that I feel I can handle with the children. Goodness knows he has enough problems at work, and to come home to face more—well, I just protect him as much as I can. My needs seem so unimportant when you consider the godly responsibilities he has to deal with all day long."

Do you realize that in your zeal to "protect" your husband from family involvement, you are allowing him to abort his God-ordained duty toward his family of walking in the revealed will of God?

God has given the husband specific instructions regarding wives, children and responsibilities at home. (We'll be talking about these instructions in the chapters to come.) God's will has been revealed to your husband and to you. If you try to protect him from keeping those responsibilities, you are "aiding and abetting" him in his disobedience to God's direct instructions.

**Bill:** When a person is out of God's revealed will, there will be repercussions. These could be manifested in our personal lives through restlessness, emptiness, obsessions, or a compulsion to search for and capture something that seems to be missing in our lives. Or it could affect our relationship with our families. A husband, for instance, may not even realize that there is estrangement in his home until his children are grown and gone, and his wife has created a life of her own without him. This man is walking in what he believes to be God's will (impressed) while minimizing God's *revealed* will concerning his family responsibilities. This is one time when a Christian *must* "leave the wrong impression."

## Finding the Right Priorities

**Anabel:** We've heard stories like this so many, many times—only the job description changes. The husband may be a college professor, a doctor, an accountant, a businessman with heavy responsibilities, a truck driver, or an engineer. It isn't the job classification that matters; *disordered priorities result in disordered lives.*

**Bill:** There are three words that need to be understood if we are to adhere to our biblical priorities:
- **Volition**—the act of using the will; exercise of the will as in deciding what to do; a conscious or deliberate decision or choice.
- **Obligation**—to bind by a contract, promise, sense of duty.

- **Integrity**—incorruptibility; firm adherence to a code of moral values; quality or state of being complete or undivided.

**Anabel:** Let me give you my biblical priorities as a wife and mother. Yours will be in the same order, but with different names and details.

1. **I have a personal relationship with Jesus.**
   I am a beloved daughter, a cherished sister, a precious child, an unblemished bride, a member of God's "forever family." My goal is to *know* Him.

2. **I am a mate.**
   I am to fill my God-given role in the marriage relationship, becoming one with my husband spiritually, physically, perceptually, and emotionally.

3. **I am a parent.**
   I am the mother of Pres, Mace, Will and Wade. I am to train them. I am to present the picture of a godly woman to them, imprinting in their minds what they might seek in a mate. I am to make home a refuge, a haven, a place of safety and security for them.

4. **I am a member of an earthly family.**
   I am Anabel HOYLE Gillham. I am to honor my mother and father, expressing my devotion to them, caring for them.

5. **I am a person with God-given talents and spiritual gifts.**
   I am a counselor, author and teacher—called by God, gifted by God. I am to allow Christ to minister through me with

the gifts He has given to me. I've been a
part-time employee of Lifetime Guarantee
Ministries for many years. I find this
acceptable to Bill and to me only when we
keep the perspective that I am a part-time
LGI employee, but I'm a full-time wife
and mother. Bill's help and understanding
in this respect are absolutely necessary.

6. **I am a friend.**
   I am Anabel, a friend to some whom God
   has given especially to me. I am to love
   them, be sensitive to them, and be available to them when they need me.

7. **I am a member of a church.**
   I am a member of a very large family.
   Some of them are hurting. I am to minister to them and be a working part of this
   body.

8. **I am a witness to the world.**
   I'm to minister to the hurting masses of
   the world—a world redeemed by God
   through His beloved Son, spurned by millions. He will reach out through me to
   reveal Himself to this world.

I *volitionally* chose the first three:

1) I accepted God's plan for salvation and, in so doing,
entered into a covenant agreement with Him;

2) I chose to become a partner in a marriage relationship;

3) I chose to bring children into the world by entering
into the reproductive plan established by God.

Do you see the words, "I *chose*"? No one forced me to
become a Christian, a wife or a mother. It was a deliberate
choice. My choice.

Numbers four through eight require certain things from me as a result of *my choice* to accept and commit myself to Number One—a growing, vital, personal relationship with Christ. I have, therefore, *obligated* myself to act out these other roles and responsibilities in a trustworthy manner.

*Integrity* is now the key word. Flawless integrity. Impeccable integrity. My reputation as a person of integrity—a person who stands by her decision—is at stake with God and the people in my sphere of influence.

**Bill:** The Bible calls that "glorifying God's Name;" it simply means enhancing His reputation by the way we live our lives.

**Anabel:** The pressures of our culture increase the stress upon all of us in these treacherous last days. Every demand placed upon me seems almost to scream out that it has the right to be number one in my life! I must use the Bible as the criterion if I am to walk with God and maintain His inner peace.

**Bill:** Of course, those same priorities hold true for men as well as for women. So often we males prioritize our career as #1, instead of placing it at #5 where it belongs, below our relationship with Christ and our family. Think about it: Have you ever heard of a man on his deathbed saying, "Oh, if only I had spent more time at the office"?

If men or women choose to live in the "lower priorities" (4-8), omitting the "higher" ones (1-3), we will inevitably experience frustration. The Holy Spirit will exert pressure designed to guide us back into the proper order for our lives. That pressure can range from mild to very intense, but His motive is pure. And as we stay within these God-ordained priorities, as we love those He has given us and train them, in turn, to love, then the world will be drawn to the person of Jesus Christ through our living witness.

Through the wonderful medium of marriage, as through our very lives, we are witnesses to the world. The writer of Hebrews said, "Let marriage be held in honor among all..." (13:4a). Next to salvation, marriage is the most real relationship available to us; and in many instances throughout Scripture, the marriage relationship is a microcosm of the relationship between Christ and Christian believers. Human to human, that's as real as it gets.

# HE MADE US DIFFERENT—
# BUT WHY?

*In order to grasp the
differences between man and
woman, we need to go back to
the beginning. The Bible tells
us how God made man, how He
made woman, and what He had
in mind for their relationship
with each other.*

# — Chapter Four —

*A woman marries a man*
*thinking she can change him.*
*A man marries a woman*
*thinking she will never change.*

**Anabel:** Not long ago, we received this letter from a single woman.

*Dear Anabel and Bill,*
*The Lord impressed me greatly with what you*
*both said about our needs as men and women. I*
*applied it to how I could meet the needs of my*
*Christian brothers by esteeming them, deferring to*
*them, and respecting them, and not destroying or*

*competing with them. It's exciting how much He is
showing me in that area.*

*I am looking at it in a totally new way. Because
I know I have a need to be loved and cared for and
because I know how it destroys me when I'm not, I
now see how it is a very real need for men to be
respected and feel they can be leaned upon and
praised. Before, I only saw it as a command to
wives and husbands; but oh, the depths of our
Lord's wisdom! It can work for me right now as a
single woman seeking to be used in this way to meet
my brothers' needs.*

## Following the Manufacturer's Instructions

The sensitive, caring woman who wrote that letter was
responding to our teaching about the similarities and differences in men's and women's needs. Most people
acknowledge that men and women have different needs.
In fact entire volumes have been written on the subject.
We speak from our own experience, both as counselors
and as husband and wife. But we have a far more important source for what we have to say.

**Bill:** If you are ever in doubt about how something
should work, you'll probably refer to the manufacturer's
instructions. In the case of men and women, our Maker
has given us His Word as a sort of "Owner's Manual" to
give us understanding. In order to grasp the differences
between man and woman, we need to go back to the
beginning. The Bible tells us how God made man, how He
made woman, and what He had in mind for their relationship with each other. Genesis 2:18 says,

> *Then the Lord God said, "It is not good for the man
> to be alone; I will make him a helper suitable for*

*him.*" (The Amplified translation says "completing him." The literal rendition is "corresponding to him.")

Let's draw a picture of Adam.

God took a look at him and said, "That's not going to fly. That guy is like an eight-cylinder car that's only hitting on four. I've got to make a second person to complete him." So God made Eve, placed her with Adam, and declared that they were now "One." He went on to say that His creation was "very good," then closed up the creating shop.

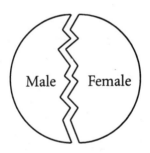

Having read this passage, let's consider an interesting question people sometimes ask: is one of these two people basically superior to the other?

**Bill:** Let's not divide up into small groups to discuss it.

Let's go to the Bible for insight to the answer.

Genesis 5:2 says,

> *He created them male and female, and He blessed*
> *them and named them* (Lit.) *Adam in the day when*
> *they were created* (emphasis added).

## Two Adams!

Did you ever notice that God made *two* Adams? Why did He do that? Because the word *Adam* means "man." God made *two* men; He made a female man to marry the mailman (guffaw). You say, "Well, that may be a great little item for the Bible Trivia game, but what does that have to do with discerning if one or the other of these two people is basically superior?" God called them both "men" implying equality. Later on He established different roles for each of them.

So where did the name "woman" come from? It came from the man God told to name everything.

As we read in Genesis 2:23:

> *And the man said, "This is now bone of my bones,*
> *and flesh of my flesh; She shall be called Woman...."*

God said, "Okay, Woman it is." He's been calling females woman ever since, but originally females were also called man.

**Anabel:** Let's look at another example to discern the original plan of equality.

> *And God created man in His own image, in the*
> *image of God He created him; male and female He*
> *created them. And God blessed them; and God said*
> *to them, "Be fruitful and multiply, and fill the earth,*

*and subdue it; and rule over the fish of the sea and over the birds...."* (Genesis 1:27-28, emphasis added).

**Bill:** God gave the marching orders to "them", not to "him". Try to be fruitful and multiply by yourself, guys. There is no evidence that the first man was out in front receiving the marching orders while the second "man" was peeking through the bushes saying, "What'd He say? What'd He say? Ask Him to speak up a little!"

## Learning to Live as One

The original plan is that husband and wife are one. God has locked Anabel and me up in a little minilab with our toothbrushes in the same glass. The lab is designed for us to learn how to *agape* each other. Sure, it's going to be tough at times. But if it were always easy, we'd never be changed into His likeness through our experiences in the lab.

Unfortunately, however, many couples don't see the process through. Today's motto is, "When the going gets tough, get going to a lawyer." That's not God's plan. That's nothing but a lord-of-the-ring escape.

**Anabel:** We certainly understand, after years of counseling, that there are extreme circumstances, such as physical abuse or child molestation, where separation should be considered. However, we are addressing the fact that many Christians are divorcing merely because they are discontented in their marriages. This may temporarily relieve the pressure, but it will never conform them to the image of Christ.

## One Picture = A Thousand Words

We have developed a diagram of a model showing the

needs of husbands and wives. This is an overview of everything we'll be talking about for the rest of the book.

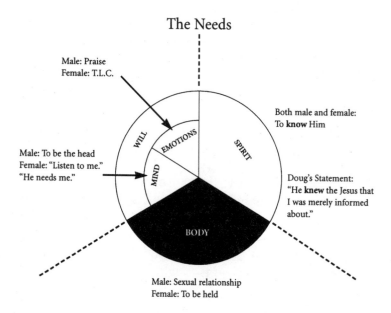

The Needs

Male: Praise
Female: T.L.C.

Both male and female:
To **know** Him

Male: To be the head
Female: "Listen to me."
"He needs me."

WILL
EMOTIONS
SPIRIT
MIND
BODY

Doug's Statement:
"He **knew** the Jesus that
I was merely informed
about."

Male: Sexual relationship
Female: To be held

As you look at our diagram, you'll notice that the areas of the spirit, soul, and body are in contrasting shades. You'll also see, by looking at the white portion of the diagram, that both husbands and wives are exactly the same in the area of the spirit in that we have one identical need—we need to know Jesus. But when we depart from the spirit area and move over into the soul, we're different.

The soul is divided into three parts—the mind, the will, and the emotions. Look first at the emotions, the lightly shaded part.

**Bill:** As a husband, I need to feel that Anabel is proud

of me. I need her to praise me. We'll talk more about the husband's specific emotional needs in the chapters to come.

## In Need of Tender, Loving Care

**Anabel:** We'll go into a wife's emotional needs more specifically in the chapters to come, too. But let's begin by saying that, as a woman, I need TLC—Tender, Loving Care.

Let me elaborate on what TLC means to me.

- **Tender** communicates gentleness. I need Bill to be tender in his touch. I need him to be tender in the way he looks at me. Sometimes a husband's eyes communicate anger or hostility or frustration. I also need him to watch the way he speaks to me. I think all wives would agree with me when I say, "Speak tenderly, please." Sometimes a man's voice can sound gruff even when he doesn't intend for it to.
- **Loving** means understanding (or at least making an effort to understand) my thoughts as well as my behavior. It means recognizing my ability to do certain things and encouraging me to do them. It also means that when he recognizes that I'm uncomfortable in doing certain things, he should not force me to do them.

  Loving also means remembering special days. Even more importantly, it means making very difficult and tedious days "special."

  For example, let's say that a wife's mother died on September 12, last year. Her husband could put an "X" on September 12 on his calendar at work. Then he might do one of several things, according to his personality and financial solvency.

He might call during the day and say, "I was just thinking about you. I know today is going to be difficult. Can you take some time to have lunch with me?" Or, "Hey, let's not cook tonight—we'll eat out." Sending flowers would be another way a husband could help to make that difficult day a special day. Flowers communicate a tender and thoughtful message. A wife will appreciate your being a part of her life in this way and it's so easy to do with a few "red X's" on your calendar.

- **Care** communicates respect. It means treating me as a person worthy of dignity and honor. Care means that Bill allows others, especially my family and my children, to see him caring for me that way. It also provides protection—the kind of protection a person would give to a very rare and precious gem. I need those things. They make me feel so special.

## A Sense of Importance

**Bill:** Moving on to another area of the soul, the mind. As a husband, I need to believe in my mind that I am the head in the marriage. That's certainly not to say that I *merit* this position. It's a need that I have and when Anabel allows me to be the head, it gives me a sense of importance in our relationship; it helps me to believe I'm needed. It allows me to believe that she can't get along as well without me. I need that. It enhances my sense of self-worth in our relationship. In short, I need to believe I'm necessary.

## A Good Listener

**Anabel:** I can understand that because I have very similar needs. I have this need for a sense of competency, for a feeling of self-worth, of importance in our relationship. I need to be needed, and I'll have all those needs met if Bill will just listen to me!

**Bill:** Just *listen* to you? Put a number on how important my listening to you is on a one to ten scale.

**Anabel:** That's a ten.

**Bill:** Now I confess that I don't understand how in the world women can get that much mileage out of their husband's listening ear! I believe most men are as much in the dark as I am about what makes a woman tick. We've got to humble ourselves and *listen* to our wives if we're ever going to learn how to make our marriages fly. The irony of it all is that they can read us like the morning paper! We must listen to our wives so we can learn how to love them like Jesus loves His wife, the Church. And remember, that word "love" means far more than the "warm fuzzies."

Now in the physical area—the body—I need a sexual relationship with my wife. And women have physical needs, too. Chapter Nine deals specifically with this part of married life, but Anabel, make a comment or two for now to give us some food for thought.

## Sex and Affection

**Anabel:** Well, women enjoy the sexual relationship, too, but there are times when we don't want that at all. We just want to be held. It makes us feel secure.

If every time I sit close to Bill on the divan, if every time I snuggle up next to him, if every time he holds me, we wind up backing toward the bedroom, I get the impression that he's not interested in meeting my needs at all. He just seems interested in getting his own needs met.

If that's the case, do you know what I may be tempted to do? Stop sitting close and stop snuggling up. Women frequently say to me, "Anabel, the only time my husband pays any attention to me is when he wants sex."

By the way, on that same one to ten scale, that's a ten, too. All of these are tens with me.

## The World and God Agree

**Bill:** It's interesting when you read a world-system book elaborating on the differences between the genders. Much of it dovetails with what God has been saying since He created the male and female and let them set up housekeeping in the Garden of Eden.

For example, the three male needs, praise, authority and a sexual relationship, all have to do with the male status, with his superiority, with his need for seeing himself as powerful and in control. That's status. And status is recognized as the main dynamic of the male lifestyle in today's culture.

**Anabel:** The needs of the woman all deal with intimacy: *tender loving care, listening and holding.* As we have so often said, women are people-centered, heart-centered creatures. They want emotional involvement...not status.

**Bill:** The man is clinging tenaciously to his *independence,* and so many of the male flesh patterns are programmed in with retaining independence as the goal...and independence is the root of all sin. We set ourselves up as "god" and declare ourselves capable of controlling our lives...very independent and very wrong.

**Anabel:** The woman is striving for *interdependence,* and she keeps evaluating the marriage relationship for closeness, needing each other, deep communication, and careful consideration of how these two lives...lived once in single-centeredness...can now be formed into one life. Key words would be considerate, kind, interested and understanding.

**Bill:** That "deep communication" that you mentioned isn't a normal part of the male makeup. Men build relationships by doing things together, not by being vulnerable. That's the way it is from the very beginning...little boys play competitive games, little girls walk around holding hands and talking. We're still doing the same thing as adults.

**Anabel:** Another major difference is that women like to sit and discuss the problem, men just want to solve it...to prove themselves...not talk about it.

There's another point for *listening* to your wife. When she talks to you about a problem, she doesn't necessarily want advice, she just wants you to know how she feels and to talk to her about it and to agree with her. Many times I've shared something with Bill and he has gone to the phone to "take care of the problem." I panic and blurt out, "Stop! Wait a minute! I don't want you to deal with the problem for me—I just wanted to share what has been going on. I needed to talk with you about it."

**Bill:** But you know, just *listening* and not taking any action would be considered weakness. Men want to step in and show their ability to "handle the situation." Then comes the exquisite joy of listening to his wife tell her friends how wonderful it is to have a husband who takes such good care of her.

Yes, the genders are unique with one exception. We have a mutual need to know Christ.

## A Mutual Need to Know Christ

These are key areas in marriage, and we're going to spend a lot of time talking about them in the following chapters. But for now, let's go back to the diagram and begin where we started, with our spirit. Both husbands and wives—in fact all men and women—have a deep need to know Jesus Christ.

## Knowing About Him or Knowing Him?

**Anabel:** When we were searching for something that would communicate "knowing Christ," we recalled an experience that we had years ago when we were involved with the Lay Witness Mission movement. When a church decides to have a Lay Witness Mission, the pastor contacts a coordinator. The coordinator provides a list of lay people who have committed themselves to that particular ministry, and have devoted their weekends to it. These men and women, in turn, go to the host church and present their Christian testimonies, bearing witness to the power of Christ in their lives.

We were involved in an LWM in Wichita Falls, Texas. Our team had arrived early on Friday, and the coordinator was helping us get acquainted with other team members. He pointed to the back of the room and said, "Doug, come up here and share your testimony with the team."

This very impressive gentleman stood up and came to the front of the room. He was impeccably dressed—a handsome man. "My name is Doug," he said. "I'm very wealthy, so much so that I became bored with taking care of all my assets and hired someone to do that for me. I decided to pursue something else in life. I went back to school and got my doctor's degree in biology, then became a professor at a university here in Texas.

"Well, soon that became boring to me, and I determined to pursue something else in life, so I decided to become a Christian. I went to the library and read a lot of books on the subject. I then aligned myself with a local church, and because of my prestige in the community, I was immediately placed on many important boards. It was no surprise to me when the pastor called one day and said, 'Doug, we're going to conduct a Lay Witness Mission in our church. Would you chair the committee to prepare for the team's visit?' And, as a matter of course, I said I would."

Predicatably, Doug did a super job in his preparation, and now the weekend had arrived when all the lay people were converging on his church. On Friday night, the church members divided up into small groups of eight or ten people, and one of the lay witnesses went with each group to a secluded area to tell of his relationship with Christ.

Doug, along with several other members of his church, was assigned to a small group. I'll let him tell the story…

"As we were walking back to our assigned room, I began to evaluate the young man who was going to be sharing with us. He was very obviously a common, laboring man. He even had oil under his fingernails as if he might have been a mechanic or something. I began to think, *I really should be in charge of this group. I am quite sure that I could handle it much more effectively than he could.*"

They got to their room, they sat down, and the young man began talking. Doug said, "As he began to share about his relationship with Christ, I became intensely aware of something: That young man *knew* the Jesus that I was merely informed about."

## Deep Water Days

**Bill:** Doug's story illustrates the point that is closest to our hearts. My dear brother, my dear sister, I have got to *know* Jesus and so does Anabel. Through our marital struggles, and through our individual lives, both of us have come to know Jesus on a deeply personal level. And this is so much more than just "head knowledge." Information will not suffice when deep waters threaten all you hold dear.

The Scriptures do not say, "*If* you pass through deep waters," but "*when* you pass through deep waters" (Isaiah 43:2, emphasis added).

**Anabel:** Deep waters come to each of us.

As counselors, and as husband and wife for many years, we do not appeal to you out of a vacuum. We don't sit in an ivory tower. We have had many "trials and tribulations," but in them all and through them all we have come to know the sufficiency of the Lord. A.W. Tozer says that after the initial experience of salvation, there comes "the glorious pursuit of knowing Him."

When it comes to the needs of men and of women, the most important need of all is spiritual. And the most important aspect of that need is knowing Christ, which takes us far beyond the assurance of a future heaven. And as we know Him, we become more aware of His presence in us. We become more able to allow Him to live His life of agape through us.

## A Picture of Christ's Commitment

**Bill:** One of my Bible heroes is Hosea; he's going to be one of the first people I hug when I get to heaven, because God has used him in my life to demonstrate two things. First, he reveals Christ's faithfulness to the Church as His beloved Bride. But, he also shows us how Christ longs for us to truly *know* Him.

Hosea typifies God's relationship to Israel, and you and I are able to relate to this, because according to scripture, Christians are spiritual Israel (Galatians 3:29; Romans 9:6-8). Hosea's relationship to his wife represents Jesus' relationship to us.

Hosea's unfaithful wife, Gomer, had a near zero commitment to her husband. Nevertheless, Hosea kept pursuing her, loving her, forgiving her, and constantly picking up the pieces of their relationship. In Chapters 1 and 2, Hosea shows how Christ patiently leads us through deep, deep waters until He is all we have left. Someone has said, "Most of us never discover Christ is all we need until He is all we have." Continually treading water will do that for you.

Through Gomer's experience, we discern that we must come to the end of ourselves if we are ever to make a marvelous discovery: Jesus is not a burdensome *Taskmaster* to us, but a loving Husband.

> *"And it will come about in **that** day [the deep water day]," declares the Lord, "that you will call me Ishi [my Husband] and will no longer call Me Baali [my Master]. And I will betroth you to Me forever; Yes, I will betroth you to Me in righteousness and in justice, in loving kindness and in compassion, and I will betroth you to Me in faithfulness. **Then you will know the Lord**"* (Hosea 2:16, 19-20, emphasis added).

## That I May Know Him...

**Anabel:** How wonderful it is to know that God can take our pain and turn it into something beautiful! I love Philippians 3:10-11 in the Amplified translation:

> *[For my determined purpose is] that I may know Him—that I may progressively become more deeply and intimately acquainted with Him, perceiving and recognizing and understanding [the wonders of His person] more strongly and more clearly. And that I may, in that same way, come to know the power outflowing from His resurrection [which it exerts over believers]; and that I may so share His sufferings as to be continually transformed [in spirit into His likeness even] to His death, [in the hope] that if possible, I may attain to the [spiritual and moral] resurrection [that lifts me] out from among the dead [even while in the body].*

**Bill:** We believe that passage is Paul's life verse. If the great Apostle Paul needed to know Christ more and more deeply, even after having been personally confronted by Him on the way to Damascus and personally discipled by Him (Galatians 1:11,12), how much more should we seek to know Him? Every one of us needs to *know* Christ, regardless of our gender or our marital status.

People sometimes say, "What you don't know won't hurt you." Well, in Christianity what you don't know will *destroy* you. It's imperative for us to understand that through Christ, God has accomplished everything necessary for us to have an intimate relationship with Him. And one thing is true, beyond the shadow of a doubt: only when our relationship with Christ is growing and thriving, will our intimate relationships with one another be the beautiful, fulfilling relationships God intends them to be.

# To Be Truly Masculine

*What is a **real** male?*
*Where can we males find*
*the ideal male role model in*
*this day and age...truly a*
*man's man?*

# —Chapter Five—

*Hmmm…now that the heavens, the earth,*
*and the living creatures are all in place,*
*let's create a human being and make him far*
*more significant than anything else We've created.*
*We'll make him in Our image, and We'll call him "man"*
(adapted from Genesis 1:26).

**Anabel:** It's no great secret that men and women are radically different, but understanding just how they differ is anything but common knowledge. With an eye toward providing some insight into what makes each gender tick, let's get down to some of the specific differences we introduced in the preceding chapter. And let's begin with males.

## Masculinity Equals Power

**Bill:** What does it mean to be masculine? As you'll recall from the description of my flesh patterns earlier in this book, I struggled for a long time to prove my masculinity so that I could accept myself. Laboring under the *feeling* that I was inferior to the macho males (but longing to be like them), I strove to *feel* like a "real" male. My stuck feeler was controlling me.

If you had observed me during high school as I related to strong, assertive girls, you would have heard me cutting them down with my sarcastic tongue; their strength motivated me to prove I was stronger than they were.

When relating to average males, I held my own fairly well. However, if a conflict occurred with one of the John Wayne types, you would have seen me passively accommodating him. Any confrontation with a powerful male was a severe setback in my effort to gain self-acceptance. Those incidents put me in my place in the pecking order, and they were painful because I interpreted them as hard evidence that I was less than a real male.

For me, masculinity equalled power. In a way, that definition is accurate. But in those days, my idea of power was fleshly—the power to outwit, to out-perform, to out-dominate any person who tried to overpower me. And because I could not consistently accomplish this, I felt like a failure.

My favorite movie plots involved an easygoing hero who patiently allowed the town toughs to push him around until he'd finally had enough. Then, with either fists or guns, he'd wipe them all out, to everyone's utter amazement. (I suspect Deputy Barney Fife might also have gone to see those movies two or three times.)

## In Search of Male Affirmation

Often a boy is not affirmed in being male (ideally, by his dad) during his formative years. To "affirm" means *to make firm; to declare positively; to assert; to confirm; to ratify; to validate.*

How should a dad affirm his son? He should spend time teaching the boy masculine activities, and developing masculine interests—talking about anything from mowing the lawn to why geese migrate. He should wrestle with him, complete with grunts and groans in the "agony of defeat" when he lets the boy win. Dads should take a genuine interest in the things which interest their sons (be it the piano, athletics, stamp collecting or fishing). Fathers should demonstrate physical love to their boys, and should frequently allow them to see warm looks of approval in their eyes. In the case of fatherless boys in the church, compassionate Christian men can make a huge contribution by acting as surrogate dads.

Experiences like these, between fathers and sons, communicate, *I like you. You are a male like me. You are of very high value to me, and I'm proud to be your dad.* At special times, a father should put a hand on his son's shoulder and say, "I thank God for the day He brought you into my life. You are a fine guy, and I am proud you're my son."

## Unaffirmed, Maladjusted Males

**Anabel:** If a son does not receive male affirmation, he doesn't realize that his dad is falling down on the job; he makes false assumptions about himself. He learns, "I am just not masculine enough. I can't accept myself. If only I were different, then I could respect myself." And because of these perceived deficits, the son develops coping mechanisms. He seeks either to correct his problem, compensate for it, or hide it from the public eye.

**Bill:** As the boy matures, he usually manifests some sort of masculinity maladjustment. His reaction may range

- From over-passivity to over-dominance.
- From homosexuality to an insatiable heterosexual appetite.
- From a massive drive to succeed to a feeling of unworthiness when success comes.
- From being too introverted to being extremely extroverted.

The fleshly responses to a lack of fatherly affirmation are as varied as the males who suffer from it.

**Anabel:** A son's lack of affirmation as a "true" male can also be the result of having a domineering mother. Since God created males to become loving leaders of their wives and families, boys need to perceive themselves as progressing toward that goal of maturity. A boy's mother is the primary female to whom he relates in his formative years. And if, as mothers, we are mega-strong and aggressive, our sons will feel intimidated. It will seem monumental, if not impossible, for them to believe they can attain a level of leadership in their own future family. The emotional results will be comparable to those Bill just mentioned.

## Choosing Fleshly Alternatives

More and more, the world is rejecting God's truth, and even some Christians are accepting radical aspects of the feminist movement as the norm. Furthermore, today's epidemic of divorce is having a devastating effect upon an entire generation of young males. Many boys are not only being reared by aggressive, man-hating, self-sufficient mothers, but they also have no father figure to affirm them as males. Consequently, they constantly struggle to affirm *themselves* as truly male.

**Bill:** I believe the subsequent frustration is the primary dynamic behind the rapid rise in homosexuality, rape, and wife abuse. This is especially evident among subcultures, such as the inner-city African-Americans, that are matriarchal in their family structure.

- Some sons give up hope of being a *real* male. Something snaps, and with a lot of help from the Deceiver the boy, *longing for the male acceptance which he cannot bestow upon himself,* opts for homosexuality.

- Other boys partially give up hope of ever being a "real" male and become passive toward all power figures, both male and female. They seek security through weakness.

- Still others overtly rebel against their mother's dominance, reject their dad (who weakly submits to his wife's power), and build a macho facade to compensate for their *feelings* of inadequacy.

These three facades, and their many variations, become fleshly identities of each male's own making as he plays "lord of the ring." They represent his vain attempts to attain self-acceptance. Those of us who have traveled any of these roads must not blame our folks, "for our struggle is not against flesh and blood, but against the rulers, against the powers, against the world forces of this darkness…" (Ephesians 6:12).

*We* are the ones who have structured our flesh patterns, not our parents. And now we must let Christ liberate us from them. But how?

## Four Steps to Your New Male Identity

**First,** we need to recognize that it was God who first infused masculine needs and traits into the male. Instead of consulting Him, we have patterned ourselves after earthly, male role models which are faulty. To solve our problem, we must repent, appropriate our new identity in Christ and begin to live as the new men we are.

**Second,** God is Spirit (see John 4:24), and He created us in His image. We are, therefore, spirit-beings. Men, think of yourself as a male spirit-critter in an earthsuit, not as a male physical-critter with a spirit. God is your spiritual Father (see Hebrews 12:9).

**Third,** when you came to Christ, you were crucified (Romans 6:6). You were then reborn as a new spirit-being in Christ and are no longer identified according to your flesh (2 Corinthians 5:14-17). In the Last Adam's lineage (1 Corinthians 15:45-48), you have a new present, a new future and a NEW PAST! Your old macho, passive or homosexual ways are NOT YOU now! They are simply your old ways (which the Bible calls "flesh," remember?), and now "we recognize no man according to the flesh" (2 Corinthians 5:16). You must set your mind on this truth...it is REALITY. Your feeler won't buy this; you must believe it with your mind solely because God says it's true.

**Fourth,** you need to find the right role model. But what is a *real* male? Where can we males find the ideal male role model in this day and age...truly a man's man? Is it the current macho screen star, football hero, or industrial tycoon? With due respect to these men, the answer is no.

## The Perfect Male Role Model

Only one perfect male has ever lived, and He was and is perfect in every way. He also implied that He is the perfect Father figure when He said, "If you have seen Me, you have seen the Father." Yes, it's Jesus. Isn't it time to adopt this perfect masculine role model, instead of emulating the imperfect ones (even Dad) in all our striving for male self-acceptance?

And that brings up an important point. We have received a false impression from artists that Jesus was effeminate. Some paintings make Him look as if He spent more time at the hairdresser than in His workshop! The God-man Jesus was a carpenter, but certain portraits depict Him as if He couldn't lift a hammer, let alone swing one all day.

No matter what His earthsuit looked like, Jesus' role as the ideal male does not rest with His muscle tone, but with His character and integrity. It doesn't matter if He stood 5'2" or 6'2", Jesus was truly masculine, and He was genuinely powerful.

## Authentic Masculine Power

By power, I don't mean His power to pump iron, walk on water or turn it into wine. I'm talking about His power to perform acts of agape. Jesus' life completely demonstrated the true definition of agape: *I will do the most constructive, edifying, redemptive thing I can do for you.*

- Jesus forgave people who burned Him. That's power.
- Jesus rescued a humiliated woman who was about to be killed by the city fathers, knowing He'd lose credibility with some of them. That's power.
- Jesus risked rejection from dear friends by confronting them. That's power.
- Jesus lived for the best "good" of others, not self. That's power.
- Jesus passed up the chance to say, "I told you so" to Peter, and fried him a fish dinner instead. That's power.
- Jesus suffered an agonizing death, although innocent, and never begged His tormentors for mercy or for a plea-bargain. He even credited them for being blind to what they were doing. That's awesome power!

Yes, true masculinity is powerful, but for what purpose? *For the purpose of obeying God and agape-loving others.* Letting Christ live through us by faith powerfully produces love, compassion, gentle but firm confrontation, patience, kindness, goodness, and integrity. It brings about a life of service, not survival. That's genuine Christ-like masculinity, modeled by the God who made us male through Jesus, who was set before us as an example. And God has *predestined* you to conform you to Christ's image (see Romans 8:29). Talk about a jump-start toward becoming truly masculine! Your spiritual Dad is already continually at work on you...His project!

## Christ, Loving Through You

Now that you're a new man, you're fully equipped to "life out" all the characteristics of true masculinity through the indwelling life of Christ. As you allow Him to, He will do it *for* you. Yes, you will fail at times. But when you fail, confess it, thank God you're forgiven, and begin again.

So, lift up your head, new male in Christ. Begin each day by affirming yourself in your mirror as the "real" man you are RIGHT NOW (even if your earthsuit looks like it needs ironing!). Allow Christ to agape those in your own house through you.

In so doing, you will grow into a mature male, and you will be affirmed in your masculinity by your True Father. You are His son (see John 1:12), and He is proud of you just because you're His. Feel His arm around your shoulders. Hear Him say to you, "You are Mine, and I am proud that you bear My Name. Today I want to express My life through you to do My will on earth. So, let's go agape 'em, son."

# WHAT DO MEN REALLY NEED?

*Males aren't all that complex
in their needs—but their needs
are very intense.*

# Chapter Six

**B**ill: When it comes to the differences between men and women, it isn't necessary to get into a debate about right-brain/left-brain thinking. Nor do we need to undertake some complicated research to uncover just what it is that men need most in their relationships with their women. Males aren't all that complex in their needs—but their needs are very intense.

It's interesting to evaluate male/female relationships that appear in Scripture. As we read about some of the characters in the Bible, we can quickly see what part the woman played—heroine or villainess—and how she either failed or succeeded in meeting her man's needs.

## A Need for Faithfulness

Samson, for instance, attracted some real losers. But then he wasn't such a winner himself. Few parents would have been excited if their daughter had brought this notorious strong man home to meet the family. Delilah was really the bad grape in his story (Judges 14-16). Samson needed a woman to be faithful to him, and Delilah sold him out to his worst enemies. He must have become pretty disillusioned with women after what he went through with her. His motto was probably...

T-R-O-U-B-L-E
That's what women have been to me!
No more women
No more strife
I was meant for the single life!

Samson had every right to be disappointed. And there are thousands of men who might sing the same song because of their unfulfilled expectations for faithfulness in the women they've loved. Husbands need wives who are faithful.

## A Need to Be Supported

**Anabel:** There are times when a husband's decision-making ability should not be questioned, and Genesis 19 records a story that describes just such an incident. Lot needed a wife who would listen to him—a woman who would follow his lead.

As you read the story of Sodom's destruction, you get the idea that Lot didn't have a great deal of authority or influence with anyone in his family. Even the young men who were soon to be his sons-in-law didn't take his warning seriously when he said, "The Lord will destroy this city." A man needs to believe that when a crisis arises, he can count on support at least from his wife—even if no one else sticks with him.

## A Need for Encouragement

**Bill:** And then there's Job. In the throes of his ongoing tragedy, the behavior of his wife is nothing short of shocking. She was either unsympathetic with him, or she failed to comprehend what he was going through (Job 1-2). Apparently, they were not of the same mind in their religious convictions, either, so it's not hard to imagine some hot word battles prior to this critical time in their lives. Job desperately needed empathy and encouragement from his wife. He didn't get it.

## A Need to Be Important

**Anabel:** Rebekah, the wife of the Patriarch Isaac (Genesis 27), was a very independent woman. She made her plans and carried them out without Isaac's input at all—some of them decidedly against his better judgment. Isaac needed a woman who would talk things over with him. Instead, he found himself married to someone who forged ahead with her own agenda, doing things her way.

And what about Adam? He needed a woman who recognized him as her spiritual leader, who would come to him and talk things over with him. "Two heads are better than one" has been true since the first man was created. How different the story of mankind might have been if Eve had said, "Well, before I eat this fruit, I think I'll talk it over with my hubby." Husbands need to be consulted before their wives make decisions.

**Bill:** On the other hand, a wife who never gives any input to her husband in his decision-making is not operating as his completer, his partner. She should give him her perspective, and he needs to give it his consideration. Women become gun-shy of this in a hurry because many men are threatened by a woman who expresses her opinion. Some men retaliate with anger if their wife comes up with a plan that might be better than the one they have generated.

The man who can't receive advice from his wife is implying that she doesn't have the intelligence to discuss important issues with him. He's also saying that he doesn't need a female to complement or complete him, that he is an island. That's degrading to her. It is also an affront to God. God does not honor "islands" who choose to live as if they do not need others.

## Appropriate Confrontation Is Agape

While we're on the issue of "talking things over," let's bring up Peter. A good wife will confront her husband about his flesh, and help him avoid "fleshing out" in public. It's like discretely telling him his pants are unzipped. He needs his wife's help. We know Peter had a wife and we know that Peter's foot was in his mouth a lot of the time. His wife knew this better than anyone else and perhaps she could have helped him temper his impulsiveness through appropriately confronting him about it.

Appropriate confrontation is a critical facet of agape love. The verse that reads, "they [husbands] may be won without a word" (1 Peter 3:1), does not mean that a wife should never point out to her husband that he's "walking after the flesh."

## "Completers" Must Take Risks

**Anabel:** As a wife, I am more aware of my husband's flesh patterns than any other person in his life. If I allow him to continue in his destructive, unChristlike behavior, then those patterns will only run deeper. Who is going to confront him if I don't?

Now, that doesn't mean that I bring up some issue six times a day—that's nagging. I broach the subject as God gives me the freedom. I pray about it, practice what I am going to say, and then, with quiet voice and apparent composure (I may be quaking on the inside with fear or anger), I point out to him his need to let Christ control him in this area. That is letting Christ agape him through me.

**Bill:** We've hit upon something here that most guys would not include on their list of "Ten Things I Want In A Wife." Hey, who would think of wanting someone to point out his flesh patterns as a basic need? However, as a man grows in Christ, and as his desire to please God increases, his heart cries out to the Holy Spirit to be an overcomer. And it's hard to be an overcomer unless he knows what he's trying to whip. We must swallow our fleshly pride and give our wives the freedom to help us identify our flesh trips.

Although having Anabel tell me that my slip is showing is not my favorite pastime, I praise God for a wife who has the spiritual guts to do so. I figure I'm a couple of rungs higher on the spiritual ladder of maturity because of this.

**Anabel:** Bill and I need to help each other, while being careful never to embarrass each other in public or before the family in order to make a point. For example, let's say that my husband has a habit of monopolizing conversations. When someone else is talking, he doesn't really listen to them; he just waits to give his version, or his thoughts about the matter. This habit can be very detrimental to friendships. It can prevent us from being included in parties or from forming close friendships.

If we're at someone's house and he pulls his everyone-listen-to-what-I-have-to-say routine, I don't choose that moment to make a remark like, "I think Tom has something to say if you'd give him half a chance!" Neither do I avoid the situation altogether. Instead, I talk to him about it later, behind closed doors. This is his flesh; he's not living according to his true identity.

**Bill:** One clear example in scripture where a woman failed to confront her husband about a very significant problem is found in Acts 5:1-10. Sapphira let down her hubby Ananias in this area. Ananias needed a woman to challenge him and help him with his flesh pattern of greed. Instead, Sapphira went along with his devious plans. *A man needs a woman with moral standards.* His respect for you as his wife may be slow in coming, in fact, he may never express it. But you will not lose your self-respect.

Just as there are bad examples, there are also some good marriages described in God's Word. For instance, look at Ruth and the respect she demonstrated for her husband Boaz. Men love that kind of respect.

In the New Testament, Aquila and Priscilla's names are always linked together. They were a team.

And Mary and Joseph became one in the truest sense of the word. They were facing life together. *A man needs that in his woman.*

**Anabel:** Let's list these qualities a man needs in his wife:

> *A need for faithfulness*
> *A need for submission to his decisions, especially*
>     *in crisis situations*
> *A need for encouragement when things go wrong*
> *A need to be consulted for advice in making*
>     *decisions and plans*

*A need to be confronted about flesh patterns*
*A wife with moral standards*
*A wife who recognizes him as her spiritual leader*
*A wife who respects him and lets others*
   *see that she does*
*A wife who is his partner in life*

All of these needs are very important to a husband's well-being. However, we believe that there are three *specific* male needs which are the most significant of all—so much so that we've devoted a special chapter to each of them. As you read through the pages that follow, you'll learn about a man's unique *need for praise.* You'll discover the truth about his innate *need to be head of the home.* And last but not least, you'll come to a greater understanding of the *need for marital physical intimacy*—a need that is deeply shared by husbands and wives alike.

Many of the things that we *do* for our husbands could be done by someone else—fixing delightful meals, taking care of his clothes, keeping the yard manicured, balancing the checkbook—but who we *are* to our husbands is reserved solely for the person he chose to fill that niche labeled "wife" in his life.

# A GOD-GIVEN NEED FOR PRAISE

*A wife can either encourage her husband as he assumes his God-given leadership role, or fight him for it.*

# Chapter Seven

Dear Bill and Anabel,

I wasn't about to cater to his giant ego! And that was my attitude—had been for 13 years. I really did think it was all just an ego problem, and I refused to play the game. Then I read your article about how the husband needs praise—that it isn't his 'giant' ego, but a God-given need—and I decided to try it.

That was two weeks ago. I've just been looking for ways to praise him, being his encourager instead of his best critic. Well, last night—for the first time in thirteen years—my husband came home and said, "You are so nice to come home to." That's what I had been yearning for. Strange isn't it? I played the game—God's way—and I won!

**Anabel:** It is so true—husbands need the praise of their wives, and it's a need that begins early in their lives. As a general rule, all children respond positively to praise. But as they get older, little boys will risk life and limb for female praise. A boy learns early on that female praise is like putting gas in his car or a match to his charcoal—he runs well and he really shines!

Sadly, many Christian women seem to do just the opposite—they've fallen into the erroneous practice of "piously" picking their husbands to pieces. Somehow they've convinced themselves that if they point out every flaw—past, present and future—the finished product will be a flawless husband. They're quick to point out weaknesses and ignore strengths. And, (this is *so* important) they forget to say "thank you" for all he does. These tactics are unbelievably debilitating to a husband's self-esteem.

## Praise Is a Ministry

**Bill:** From the very onset of male-female relations, female praise is an unequalled balm to males. The schoolboy who loves to draw pictures of trains finds himself highly motivated when one of the girls in his class stops at his desk and says, "Did you draw that? I'm impressed! I didn't know you could do things like that."

The man who loves to grow African violets finds himself flushed and excited by the female friend who says, "Oh, I dearly love African violets! Would you have time to show them to me?"

A female high school teacher brags on her motley crew of boys and their test results astound the principal. "How did you get them settled down to do this kind of work?"

"Oh, I just praised them."

## Valid Praise, Not Flattery

**Anabel:** Bill's buttons pop off when I say such things as, "You amaze me! You can fix just almost anything!"

He needs to feel that I am proud of him. He needs my praise, and he even has a scriptural explanation for his need. He laughingly says that he loves to hear me read it out of the Amplified translation because it "goes on and on with lots and lots of verbs."

> ...And let the wife see that she respects and rever-ences her husband—that she notices him, regards him, honors him, prefers him, venerates and esteems him; and that she defers to him, praises him, and loves and admires him exceedingly.

**Bill:** I love it! What a marvelous truth from God's Word! I've asked Anabel to needlepoint it and frame it for my office, but for some reason she seems never to have enough time to get around to it....

The fact is, we men need female praise. But we don't need flattery. The Bible says that "Flattery is a form of hatred and wounds cruelly" (Proverbs 26:28 TLB). It's not that we have an ego problem although admittedly, some guys overdo it. God created all males with a specific need for female praise. We were born with it just as females were born with a need for male TLC.

## "Hey Mom!"

Let me illustrate. Here's a little six-year-old kid. He's hanging by his heels from a limb in the apple tree in his back yard. Who does he yell at to come out and see him? Mom! "Hey, Mom! C'mere!"

He's trying to demonstrate to the main female in his life what a "hoss" he is and that he can do a physical, masculine thing she can't do. He wants her to be astounded at his daring! If she steps to the door and says, "Wow! How can you stay up there like that? Aren't you afraid you'll fall?" it thrills him to death. Guys love that sort of thing. It makes us feel male. We come factory-equipped that way.

**Anabel:** Can you imagine what would happen if I were that little boy's mom and I decided to go out and demonstrate my expertise as a "tree-hanger" and out-performed him?

I doubt that he could verbalize his feelings at that age, and every boy is different. One son might be disappointed at having been bested by "his woman" and lose interest in climbing trees. Another might grit his teeth and vow he'd learn to hang by one foot in order to outdo me. But you can see that it's just not wise for a mom to consistently demonstrate that she is equal to or better than her sons as they test their masculine wings.

**Bill:** That's right. It will impact the boys' flesh patterns, giving them "masculinity hang-ups." Let's look in on the same boy at age ten or so. He's weaning himself off Mom, and developing an interest in ten-year-old girls. He can't hang in the tree and holler, "Hey girls, look!" That would be uncool. So instead, when he sees the girls approaching, he gives them his best tree-hanging routine complete with sound effects to attract their attention. Then he imagines that they are thinking the same thoughts Mom used to express: "Wow, look at that!" He gets that same good feeling, and it reassures him that they think he's a hunk.

Once he's in high school, the whole process gets more sophisticated, so tree-hanging is out. High school women expect something more spectacular, so our young man becomes an athlete. He sweats blood on the football field, and when he finally gets his letterman's jacket, he practices looking, walking and acting cool in front of the mirror. Once he gets all this down pat, he strolls down the halls of the high school in his jacket and basks in the admiring glances of the girls. That's what pom-pom girls are all about! The girls know it's a game and so do the guys. We've all played it. It's the way God made us.

Hey, when the camera zooms in on the guy who scored in an NFL game, what does he say? "Hi, Mom!" I know he's putting us on, but he doesn't say, "Hi, Dad," does he? It bears repeating—we males need female praise, especially from the female we love.

## Foolish Words, Wise Words

**Anabel:** I remember sunning myself at a swimming pool one day. Two young couples were the only other people there. Apparently, one couple had a pretty comfortable relationship, but the other kids were just becoming acquainted. The boy went over to the diving board and called to his girlfriend to come with him—she was a cute little thing. She slid into the pool and swam over. He perched on the end of the board and kept bouncing. He was waiting until all eyes were on him before he began his exhibition. I even heard him mumble under his breath, "You all better watch me."

Finally he dived in, giving a passing-fair performance.

Without a word, the girl climbed out of the pool and onto the board. She poised on her toes for a moment, then executed a beautiful dive, hardly making a splash as her slender body entered the water.

As they climbed out of the pool together, I heard the guy say, "Let's go play some basketball...."

## When the Letterman's Jacket Is Long Gone

**Bill:** I can identify with that. Anabel has always praised me, even during those years when I was giving her such misery. It's really been amazing. One night I was up late reading and she was already in bed. I tried to be as quiet as possible as I slipped into my side and eased the covers up, not wanting to disturb her. But she was awake.

She reached over, patted me on the hip and said, "I'm so proud you're my husband." You talk about feeling ten feet tall. To have that sweet woman say something like that to me makes me feel like a king.

On another occasion, a man offered to let our family use his lakeside cottage in Canada for a two-week vacation. After one second's laboring in prayer, I felt led to accept it! God wants all His children to vacation in Canada, right? So we went, and one afternoon Anabel was sitting out on the deck doing her needlework. Her thimble slipped off her finger, dropped through a crack in the boards, and disappeared into the lake. She went into the cabin, rummaged around until she found another thimble, and went back to her sewing. This time I was sitting on the deck with her. The thimble came off again, hit her leg and was heading for the water. I reached out from my chaise lounge, picked the thimble out of the air and handed it back to her.

She smiled at me and said, "Your coordination just amazes me!"

Hey, I love that kind of stuff! I was telling that story in one of our live seminars, and at the break a man came up to me and said, "Man, if my wife would say things like that to me, I'd dive in after that other thimble!"

## Sgt. Sin's Lie: "I'm Unworthy of Praise"

On the other hand, I've learned that some guys can't

relate to these examples. When I talk to certain males about their need for their wife's praise, thoughts come into their mind like, *I wouldn't want my wife to tell me I'm coordinated. Now, Gillham is different. He probably goes for that, but I don't.*

Those thoughts are not being generated in his "sound mind," in his "new creation" mind (1 Corinthians 2:16b); they're being served up to his mind by the power of sin (Romans 7:23).

If you are ever to be an overcomer, it's imperative that you understand that the battle which rages in your mind is not a *civil* war, but a *bipartisan* war. While it *seems* that your mind wages war against itself (the "bad you" against the "good you"), in reality *it does not.* A "mind of Christ" does not generate evil thoughts (1 Corinthians 2:16b, 1 John 5:18).

Remember, the power called *sin* which wages war against your mind is a personified noun (*represented as a person* [ref. Vine in Chapter One]) whom I have nick-named "Sgt. Sin." He's none other than the Deceiver's secret agent through which he launches the thought-missles that you experience via first-person, singular pro-nouns (I, me, my, etc.) every waking moment.

This is how you are deceived into "doing the very thing [you] do not wish," when in reality "[you] are no longer the one doing it, but sin [the personified noun] which dwells in [you]" (Romans 7:19,20). These thoughts *seem* as though they're your ideas ("*I* think I'll add this to my expense account; the boss'll never know"), when in fact, your sound mind *received* them from Sgt. Sin, the Deceiver's agent, and you *chose* to make them your own and then carried them out. *You* sinned, but you did not generate the idea.

Listen: *The only way the Deceiver can get you to sin is by fooling you into choosing to accept those thoughts—then and only then do they become your thoughts, and then—through your choice—you sin.*

**Anabel:** Bill and I believe that a Christian husband who rejects praise from the woman he loves is being deceived by the power of sin. Somehow during childhood, probably because of the conditions he encountered in his home life, he began to consider himself unworthy of praise. His emotions reacted accordingly and now they are stuck. Today, if he receives a compliment, he *feels* unworthy of it, he *feels* uncomfortable hearing it. Or he assumes that the giver is a phony, or undiscerning, or has a hidden motive.

**Bill:** Even though this man has received Christ into his life, Sgt. Sin (the Deceiver's agent) works continually through his flesh. Sin blocks him from being able to receive his wife's praise—or any one else's praise—that God intends for him to have.

He is being blocked by his stuck feeler, embracing Sin's lies: "Man, 'I' am really a loser." The solution to this problem lies in understanding his true identity. The man who cannot receive praise must learn to accept himself as a *new*, changed, re*creation* in Christ Jesus and learn to allow Christ to receive the wife's praise for him.

## A Thought-Provoking Equation

**Anabel:** Here's an interesting comparison: someone has equated the emotion a woman experiences when her husband is having an affair to the emotion a man experiences when his wife refuses to praise him. At first you might react, "No way do those compare, Anabel." Oh, but they do.

You see, if my husband were to seek out another woman, what he is essentially saying to me is this: "Your femininity is simply not pleasing to me. I am going to find someone whose femininity pleases me."

What I am saying to my husband when I do not praise him is: "Sorry, but your masculinity just is not pleasing to me. Quite frankly, I see nothing in you to praise."

One time we were doing our seminar in Georgia. A lady wrote this note to me; I've since asked her permission to share it.

> I sat in the seminar listening as though you were speaking directly to me as you spoke of the "strong woman." I am a strong woman. I was raised by my divorced mother who was the epitome of independence and strength. Need a man? Ha! Boy, that was not part of the program. Need a man to make a decision? Are you kidding? I am an independent, strong-willed performer, though I don't look it. I'm 5'2", 105 lbs. But I have a will of iron, and it is ruining my life. There is a constant power struggle between my husband and myself.
>
> I'm saved and I've read the Scriptures, but they did not sink in. God spoke to me last night when you said someone compared the emotions a woman has (knowing her husband has had an affair) to the emotions a man has when he does not get praise from his wife. I could not believe my ears! You see, I never praise my husband. I always think: "He can't make a decision that is right."
>
> Last night I had a dream. I dreamed that my husband had an affair. And I mean I dreamed the details. I actually felt the emotions as if it were true. It hurt so badly! I woke up at 4:30 a.m. sobbing. At that point I realized what I was doing! Anabel, God began a work in me!

## Years of Emptiness

In one of our counseling sessions we were talking with a couple who had been married for thirteen years. They were together in the room, and at the height of the man's tirade, he turned to his wife—with all the vehemence he could muster, with all of the hostility built through the years—and he said to her, "Never, my *dear* wife, never in thirteen long years of marriage did you *ever* praise me in front of anyone!"

Perhaps you are prone to mutter, "Big Deal. Bless his poor, little heart." Well, yes. Bless his heart, because you see, God has placed in every husband a need for female praise. And He has given me to my husband to meet that need.

**Bill:** You know, it breaks my heart to hear one of my sisters in Christ make disparaging remarks to her kids about their dad's qualifications as a man or as the leader of the family. I just ache for the poor guy, imagining what it would be like to be in his shoes. No one can ever know how many times I thank God for giving me a woman who would never undermine me like that with my sons.

**Anabel:** During a seminar in California, a man came up to me and said, "Anabel, may I talk to you for a minute?" He was an older gentleman, and it was interesting to me that he was twisting his hat in his hands as he talked.

We isolated ourselves and he began. "Anabel, you know the story you told about the man whose wife did not praise him for thirteen years?"

"Yes," I said. He looked down at his hat, twisted it a little more, and when he looked up, his eyes were tear-filled. He looked back down, regained his composure and then said, "Would you believe thirty-nine years, Anabel?"

"I beg your pardon?"

"Yes, thirty-nine long years."

## Obedience, Not Flattery

You might ask, "Wouldn't she be a phony if she began to praise her husband if she didn't feel that he was worthy of it? Wouldn't that make her a hypocrite?"

No, it would not. You can go to a seminar on marriage and come home with your arms loaded with books and your brain loaded with good intentions, but instead of becoming the "Total Woman," in two weeks you're the "totalled" woman. You simply can't do it unless you know how to trust Christ to do it all for you, through you. I have had women rather irately say to me, "Look, Anabel. I'm not playing games. My husband is a loser, a real loser. I'm not going to make up things to praise him for."

Each time this happens, I explain, "My dear sister, when you praise your husband, you are not 'playing games'; you are being obedient. You won't be 'making up' things to praise him for; you'll be trusting the Holy Spirit within you to show them to you. They'll be valid things, not flattery. You will be meeting a need, a God-given need, for your husband."

**Bill:** Our son, Pres, makes the following statement in his teaching: "Encouragement should be for small things as well as large things. It should not be limited to performance tasks that are well done. Characteristics, attributes, desires, and admirable qualities are all good objects for encouragement. This perspective will act to build up the person for who he *is* as opposed to what he has done."

## Proverbs for Praise

**Anabel:** I love Ken Taylor's paraphrase of the Proverbs. Let me share some that emphasize the husband's need to feel that his wife is proud of him.

*A nagging wife annoys like constant dripping. A father can give his sons homes and riches, but only the Lord can give them understanding wives* (Proverbs 19:13b-14).

*A worthy wife is her husband's joy and crown* (Proverbs 12:4a).

By my behavior, I can become a "crown" for my husband:
- My children will see him as king.
- The people around me will see him as king.
- I bestow on him all of the rights, responsibilities, and honors of a king.
- He will see himself as king.

When I crown my husband with praise, he is secure in his position. He is not threatened, and so he is neither forced to overly compensate by being domineering or sarcastic, nor is he required to abdicate his role because of a lack of confidence. A wife becomes her husband's crown through her attitude, her behavior, and her interaction with him and everyone else in the home.

Let's go on with the verses from Proverbs; remember, "a worthy wife is her husband's joy and crown." Now listen carefully to this:

*The other kind corrodes his strength and tears down everything he does* (12:4b).

*It is better to live in the corner of an attic than with a crabby woman in a lovely home* (21:9).

*Better to live in the desert than with a quarrelsome, complaining woman* (21:19).

## Fourteen Off-Ramps Leading to Love

Here are fourteen very practical ways to express love to your husband. If you are performing eleven or more of these very simple acts, it isn't necessary to define love to feel sure that you love your husband, and he knows that you love him. With fewer "Yes" answers, you may still love him, but he probably doesn't *feel* certain. Finding more ways to show your love might add new meaning to marriage for him.

1. Tell your husband often that you love him.
2. Plan menus around his tastes.
3. Have some endearing name for him.
4. Eagerly prepare for his daily homecoming.
5. Delight in his praise of you.
6. Like to make him smile.
7. Want him always to look his best.
8. Comfort him when he feels bad.
9. Often think how wonderful he is.
10. Miss him when he's away on trips.
11. Praise his good qualities to your friends.
12. Gladly try to match his moods.
13. Do your best to please him.
14. Feel closer to him as time passes.

## Christ in You, Enabling You

*A wife can either encourage her husband as he assumes his God-given leadership role, or fight him for it.*

There is no way that any woman can do what is required of her in her marriage. But as a wife allows Jesus Christ, who indwells her, and who is now her very Life (Colossians 3:4), to perform through her, He will meet this need in the husband—beautifully!

There is such victory available to us as we apply the truth of the "exchanged life" (our life for Christ as Life) to our marriages. There is such hope in the reality: "Christ in you, the hope of glory." Jesus wants to do it all *for* us. But we must cooperate with Him in order to experience the amazing transformation that can take place. We must choose the way of the cross. We must "take up our cross daily" and "offer ourselves as a living sacrifice." Then, and only then, can Christ love our spouses—and praise them—through us.

# BORN TO BE A GODLY LEADER

*Submission is a **ministry** to our husbands;
when we view it that way, it becomes more
palatable as opposed to being obligatory.*

# Chapter Eight

Dear Bill,

Pat and I have been separated now since March 23rd. We see each other about once a week, but we don't get much accomplished. From my point of view, she builds my hate and resentment toward her by being so "bossy." It seems like she's on my back constantly about how I'm failing, and I just take it and take it; then finally, before I do something that I know I'll be sorry for later, I leave.

She says she lost respect for me because I didn't make decisions, but when I did, she would not go along with them unless they were identical to what she wanted to do or what she thought ought to be done. She would either ridicule me or run me down. If it was really *important, she would lose her temper and tear something up.*

*How, as I've asked her so many times, do you win in a situation like that? Maybe I went about making decisions in the wrong way, maybe I was too dogmatic or something. But I simply don't understand how to deal with her.*

**Bill:** Husbands need to believe that they are the head of the marriage relationship, and this letter illustrates the point powerfully. But, before we begin to look at the mistakes women make in this area, let's begin by acknowledging the fact that I and many other males have blown it, and our marital relationships have suffered. The ways and means husbands sometimes use to gain submission from their wives can devastate and destroy their marriages. Christ through me will not act that way to Anabel.

## Winning Your Wife With Kindness

Too often men have the attitude, "Male redbirds are prettier than female redbirds; I'm bigger than you are; I can throw a rock straighter than you can; I know which way is north; therefore, you ought to recognize me as your authority." That goes over like a lead balloon with wives, and no small wonder!

My friend Russ Kelfer makes these points to husbands concerning submission: "No place in Scripture do we read, 'Husband, see that your wife submits to you....' One of the great deterrents to wifely submission and one of the great boons to the liberated women's movement, has been the autocratic, unloving, insensitive clod known as the evangelical Christian husband. The matter of submission is between a woman and God. The husband's role is to love (agape) her so much and so consistently that she is drawn irresistibly into the holy condition known as submission."

Consider the man who is the head of a firm and has employees with various job descriptions. To what extent will he go in order to develop a successful company with a loyal, contented and productive work force? How does he motivate his employees to carry out his directives? What would some of his leadership responsibilities include?

- Establish safe and efficient working conditions
- Use sound, motivational techniques
- Provide health care
- Establish good relationships with employees
- Be mindful of the emotional needs of each employee
- Provide vacation time
- Delegate duties within the bounds of the job description
- Practice constructive criticism and encouragement
- Be consistent as a leader of integrity and fair treatment

If the head of the firm were to incorporate all of these qualities into his leadership style, he would never need to demand, manipulate, or threaten anyone. Instead, because of his altruistic attitude and his overt sense of responsibility to achieve the greater welfare for all, a general desire to do the very best possible work would pervade the corporation. Husbands need to apply these same motivational steps in their "headship" position.

## Responsible, Not Dictatorial

**Anabel:** I like the word responsibility. The husband is *responsible* for his home and the people under his care. But imagine how frustrating it would be to have responsibility such as that, and to have no one recognize your position. It would be like being PTA president but no one calls you, no one informs you, no one listens to you or does what you say.

Those same uncooperative people are still expecting you to organize open house events and plan money-raising projects! How many times I have rebelled (in thought more than in actions) when I thought Bill was trying to *control* me, when in reality he was only trying to *care* for me.

Still, many men interpret "head" as "dictator." That's not what it means, and it's no wonder that a wife will resist being under submission to a threatened, insecure husband who must have the first, last, and middle say in order for his flesh to be satisfied.

**Bill:** A husband must not act like some fanatical autocrat, demanding, "You submit to my authority!" "You do as I say!" "Don't you dare question my decisions!" He's not a general; he's a gentle leader. And, as he fulfills his responsibilities as leader of the family, he will be more likely to find the results he's seeking: partnership, compatibility, unity, loyalty, and respect.

## A God-Given Leadership Role

Anabel has earned a "10" in the praise category. But I'm not going to give her a 10 on this one. Her lack of submission to my headship and my subsequent domineering attempts to control her caused us to experience what she labels as, "That blissful state of marriage called 'hell on earth.'"

Those days are forgiven, and she has come to see me as a man with a void that only she can optimally fill. God created me this way. It isn't that I'm such a red-hot leader, that I *merit* her submission or that I'm on a big ego trip, but I was created to be the head of something, and as my wife, Anabel is elected.

Just because I was created by our Father to be the head doesn't mean that I am any better than she is. It's just that we were created with different roles to "life out" on Planet Earth. Anabel and I are to fit together as one, and to do that, we must work at meeting one another's needs.

**Anabel:** It takes the sting out of submitting to Bill when I see in Scripture that I am his equal. Our relationship is the same as Jesus' is to the Father. Jesus is the Father's equal, but He totally submits to the Father's authority over Him (Philippians 2:6-8 and 1 Corinthians 15:28). They're equal, but They each have different roles to carry out in Their relationship.

Some wives choose to resist their God-ordained role and try to control their husbands. The following is an excerpt from a husband's letter which illustrates the point clearly.

> *It's a vicious circle! Janice runs our house, but doesn't really want to. It's impossible to satisfy her! Her need for precision and order is never ending, and my ability to perform at all levels is inconsistent according to her standards. She then believes that our relationship is unbalanced and doesn't feel capable of giving me the things I desperately need at that particular time. I start to feel rejected and unacceptable to her as a husband and father, and wind up seeking acceptance somewhere else…in the arms of another woman. I hate it, but I simply don't know how to change things.*

## Searching for Esteem

**Bill:** I remember a couple I saw years ago. They were both born-again, but when the guy confessed that he'd had eleven affairs (count 'em!), they decided it was time to come in for counseling.

One day the wife came to see me by herself. She arrived late, explaining that her car had been difficult to start. When I asked how she had managed to get the car running, she said, "I raised the hood, removed the breather, freed up the automatic choke, put the breather back on, and it kicked right off."

I said, "You're kidding!"

She said, "Oh, no. When anything goes wrong, I fix it. Last week the element burned out in my oven. I flipped the breaker off and removed the element, went to the electric shop and bought a replacement, installed it, turned the breaker on and was back in business. Believe me, if I waited around for that louse to fix things they never would get done."

I said, "You're not going to like what I've got to tell you. I agree that your husband has blown it royally, but you are a major part of the problem. Because you are so self-sufficient, you are making him feel that he's unnecessary. Your strength makes him believe you can get along better without him than you can with him."

Of course, the guy was guilty eighteen ways from Sunday (eleven actually) for what he had been doing. I'm not minimizing that, but let's consider his male needs. We'll get to female needs later on, so bear with us. The guy was out there in those foreign beds trying to *feel* like he was attractive and necessary to a woman. He was desperately seeking affirmation that he was truly masculine.

Was he sinning? Yes. Was his behavior excusable? Certainly not. Is he accountable for his sinning? Yes. But what was motivating the man? What was the Deceiver capitalizing on? The man's wife had made him feel that he was unnecessary in his own home.

**Anabel:** Home to some men means insecurity, to others it means failure.

To others bedlam…or hostility…or pressure.

Home means rejection of what they say…

rejection of what they do…

rejection of who they are;

And the role that we wives play in our husbands' images of home cannot be overemphasized.

## The Case of the Unmotivated Woodworker

**Bill:** I took two years of shop in high school because the football coach was the teacher, and I came out with a billy club and a little gun rack—not too swift. After graduation I went cold turkey on woodworking. However, at about age thirty or so, I began to believe that I could make things out of wood. Woodworking seemed macho to me, so I was kind of eager to give it another try. Success would feed my masculine needs.

I bought a saber saw and some wood and whipped out a little shelf. I gave it to Anabel, we hung it on the wall and put her little trinkets on it. When company came over, she'd say, "Look what my smart husband did." I'd try to act cool, but inside I was loving it. So, I became a prolific shelf-maker. My shelves are all over our house now.

I milked that deal till it ran dry, and then retired from shelf-making. You know, you can never satisfy the flesh, and all of this was a flesh trip to get my need for masculine self-esteem met, not to make shelves for Anabel.

The years went by, and one day Anabel said, "Bill, I need you to make another shelf for the boys' room."

Now, I didn't understand that she was actually saying, "Husband, love me one more time like you used to." I thought she was asking me to make a shelf! I had been there...done that. It didn't excite me anymore, so I ignored her. A month went by, and she asked me again. I still ignored her. Another month, another request. I ignored her again.

One afternoon I came home from the office and she said, "Hi! I've got a surprise for you!" She took me by the hand, led me back to the boys' room, and there on the wall was a new shelf she had made, and *it looked as good as mine.* Something died in me when I saw that shelf. I don't recall how I responded; I probably remarked that it looked nice, but I was downcast inside. Years later as I was counseling, the Lord brought that episode to mind and gave me understanding as to what had happened to me.

When I saw Anabel's shelf, it made me feel as if she could get along just as well without me as with me. It communicated that she didn't really need me.

**Anabel:** And so often we are asked, "All right. What *should* that woman have done?" There are men to whom that would be no threat at all. Go right ahead and build the shelf! This is a rare breed, however.

Most men sense great fulfillment when they "fix it," or "build it." It somehow reinforces this innate need to be in control and competent. They are able to dominate their world of "things." And, of course, most men get a lot of pleasure in showing their expertise and strength in any arena because of the praise and admiration they receive.

But if you are married to a man who is threatened by your ability and strength as Bill was in our relationship, then you can expect repercussions when you exceed or equal his ability to perform in what he perceives to he *his* arena. Put yourself in his place and try to understand what would be happening to you if he deliberately aggravated one of your flesh patterns. Ideally, the two of you can communicate and work together on this problem.

If you are married to a man who has passive flesh he'll sit back and let you build the house! In either case, you need to talk about those things that are so obviously flesh and not Christ expressing life through him. Just remember, when you point out his flesh faults, be prepared to let him have his "pound of flesh" from you, too.

So what do you do? You communicate about why you

need the shelf and how you view it as "loving you," and as we have said before, quantify (on a one to ten scale) just how important this is to you. This would give him hard data on evaluating your need for a new shelf. Above all, be sure you are allowing Christ to live through you.

## Strong Women, Weak Marriages

**Bill:** What about you? Did God create you as a new woman in Christ who believes in her own strength, her own talent, her own wisdom, her own ability...in you, yourself and you? No, you are the product of a "planned spiritual pregnancy." You were re-created in Christ. Hey, this isn't my idea; check this all out against the Scriptures. Note in Ephesians 2:10 that you were "created in *Christ* for good work," not in your *mother*.

**Anabel:** Where did your assertiveness come from? Perhaps you had to be strong in order to survive, so you *developed* strength. Perhaps you were reared by strong people and the key to their acceptance and to your own self-acceptance was to be strong. You may have gained acceptance by playing "lord of the ring" then. But it's all flesh now.

Of course, we are to be strong...but "strong in the Lord, and in the strength of His might" (Ephesians 6:10)...not in ourselves. And that strength in Him enables us to submit when we don't feel like it; His strength gives us the power to hold our tongue and not be bossy and domineering. His strength gives us the power to love when we don't feel loving; to serve when we don't want to serve; to humble ourselves and say "I'm sorry" when it isn't really our fault. His strength and the strength that you programmed in because of your private world are at polar positions. Your strength is offensive to Him. Only His strength through you is acceptable.

**Bill:** We have found that a woman who has assertive, aggressive flesh is probably not married to a man who is stronger than she is. Her husband usually has passive flesh or macho flesh. If it is the former and they're twenty years into marriage, her constant prayer is, "Lord, dynamite this guy off the divan and get him involved in this home. He just sits there and says, 'Go ask your mom.'" If it's the latter, then there is probably a hot war on land, sea, and in the air. He may be insulting her with cutting remarks in front of friends, family, and even checkout clerks. She is the object of open ridicule, or at best, sarcastic barbs. There may have been affairs over the years, even though her husband is one of the superstars in the church.

How do I know? Because that describes hundreds of counselees as well as Bill and Anabel (with the exception of the affairs). But, praise God, He has turned things around for us through the truths we are offering to you in this book.

Here's some loving advice—if you are married to a threatened male, don't compete with him! Don't beat the daylights out of him in Ping-Pong, badminton, croquet, etc. He'll take up winter camping—above timberline. He will freeze you out. He'll be forced to try to accomplish some macho thing you can't beat him at. Don't consistently kill him in bridge, hearts, or anything else (if you know he'll never beat you, you'd be wise not to play in the first place!), or he'll take up an individual hobby and insist you go to parties without him.

**Anabel:** I remember teaching one summer at a Christian athletic camp. As I shared this concept these very successful, high-achieving young women athletes crowded around after the session with this question: "So should we refuse to play games or compete in sports? Should we pretend to lose? That's just not right!"

Once again, your husband may be able to handle your besting him in such settings. I'm going to have to be honest and say that I have encountered very few. In the early years of marriage they might say, "That's my wife! Isn't she something?" But as the years roll by the resentment builds. and if you have children it can be very detrimental to them to see their mom beating their dad.

You'll produce a "strong as garlic" daughter who emulates your strength. Or a threatened son who doesn't have the same make-up as his dad. The wreaths you receive for your outstanding performance could create the chains that your sons or your daughters will find controlling their lives.

Having a scrapbook filled with mementos of yor achievements or a shelf filled with victor's trophies does little to placate a broken heart. Remember your job classification has one major area: *Christ is your life and allowing Him to express that life through you is your highest achievement and your greatest trophy.*

## No Winners in Competitive Christianity

**Bill:** Here's an even more devastating problem—this appeal from husbands breaks our hearts: "Dear wife, don't compete with me in your Christianity, or I'll quit going to church with you. You attend two Bible studies each week. You've got your memory verses stuck all over the house. You've got five Bibles—all underlined—and one lying open on the coffee table hoping I'll read it. I hear you talking to your prayer partner on the phone, and you sound like a King James Bible. You use words like 'quicken' and 'tarry.' Hey, nobody says tarry anymore—we make bathrobes out of that stuff! Becoming a Christian while living with you scares me to death."

If that sounds like your husband could have written it,

and he happens to accept Christ, chances are he'll be a closet-Christian until you eject from your earthsuit. He's not going to put himself into one more competitive situation with you. As a new believer, he'd have to begin on a bicycle with training wheels while you're already in a Mercedes loaded with gas.

If your fleshly strength is your security, you may think you'd die if you were to lose it. Instead, it's precisely the thing the Holy Spirit is trying to put to death in order that Christ might *become* your strength. Learn from Gideon. God states flat out that the reason He whittled Gideon's army down from 32,000 to 300 was so they'd be too weak to take credit for the victory He was about to give them (Judges 7:2). Will you swap your human strength for His strength...made perfect in your weakness? Tell Him that's what you want. The refining process won't be easy, but you'll love the results.

## Comfortable in an Upside Down World

**Anabel:** Sometimes men and women become accustomed to their reversed roles. Take Bill's folks, for instance. His mom was very definitely the leader. But if we could have talked with her about their "upside-down relationship," I daresay Mom would have said, "But I enjoy taking the lead. I've always been a forceful, aggressive, competent person. I don't mind the role of leader. I'm very comfortable with it."

And if we could have interviewed Pop on the subject, he would have said, "Oh, she likes to make decisions and confront people. I don't. She's always been in charge around here, and I like it that way."

You may be in the same kind of upside-down marriage asking, "Why should we change if we like it? We're both comfortable in our roles. Why make waves?"

**Bill:** We're back to the law of gravity again. When a marriage is set up so that the wife is "lifing out" the role of husband by being the authority figure, and the husband is "lifing out" the role of wife by submitting to his wife's authority, as I said before, something is going to go *splat.* Something will suffer, be it the marriage, the kids, or the grandkids, because we cannot violate God's ways without running into problems. But remember, His ways are all for our good (see Romans 8:28-29), so change is well worth the effort. It will pay both present and eternal dividends.

**Anabel:** Perhaps the best way to demonstrate this point is to allow a competitive wife to share her experience with us. The following letter from a friend is a dramatic illustration of this type of marriage. The eventual result found this dear woman being transferred, against her will, into the single-again group:

> *Dear Anabel,*
> *Do we ever fit the former Gillham family portrait. What an unbelievable mess. Hell on earth created so quietly under a roof in a house that appeared to be a home to the world looking in.*
>
> *One of our biggies has been competition. I have beaten him in every physical activity we have ever participated in. I took up bicycling a couple of years ago and worked at it diligently. A two-hundred-mile ride in two days was a recreational trek! I'd think he was a real cream puff because he couldn't whip off twenty-five miles (just a stroll for me) without being worn out.*
>
> *Tennis? Oh, yes. I could wipe him off the court. I practiced diligently, took lessons, and had a lot of natural ability. I couldn't wait to get him on the court and show him how good I was.*

*Last year we got a twenty-five foot sailboat. He had dreamed of this boat and spent months reading how to maneuver and sail it. You know, it takes a bit of expertise to put it in the slip without scraping the sides or bumping the bow. Well, guess who qualified as an expert...first try? I did do one thing smart, Anabel. I never tried to sail it while he was on board. Oh, I've really proven myself in many areas, unfortunately, none of them encouraged my husband to want to spend any "fun" time with me.*

## "Next Time, I'll Win"

We went to see them as quickly as we could and talked with her first. She was well aware of what had happened and desperately wanted the chance to try again. Then we went to see him. We weren't quite sure about his address, so he met us at a designated parking lot—in his Porsche.

We followed him to his very nice bachelor pad. He took off his suit coat, loosened his tie, and offered us refreshments. As we talked, he listened very politely, and when we had finished, he said to us, "You have no idea how I appreciate your love and your interest. But I have no intention of getting back in the marriage, no intention at all." He paused, "But if I ever should, I'd win next time."

How heartbreaking.

So many stories—from real people. We once attended a meeting as conferees. One of the most attractive couples at the conference wound up sitting with us in a relaxed atmosphere. He was a very successful businessman. She was his counterpart as a successful businesswoman.

He talked about his clients, and she talked about her clients. They seemed to complement each other so nicely. One morning before the conference ended there was a knock at our hotel door. It was the husband, and we asked him in. Before we could start any small talk, he blurted out, "I'm leaving my wife."

We looked at each other, then at him and said, "What in the world?"

Neither of us will ever forget his answer: "Mary doesn't need me. She will do just fine without me. I have found a woman who needs me."

## "A Woman Who Needs Me"

**Bill:** This is so common today. How subtly the enemy is eroding the home. Even the TV sitcoms send us the message. I'm sure you remember "The Cosby Show"; in it the Huxtable males are portrayed as laid-back, jovial, and easygoing, while the females are depicted as aggressive and assertive. In a head-to-head conflict over a major family issue between the females and the males in their household, who would you put your money on?

**Anabel:** How many files do we have—files with tragic stories inside? How many cases where a man has left a very efficient, capable, independent, strong-willed woman for "a woman who needs me"?

It isn't that a man falls out of love with one woman and in love with another. Instead, he finds frustration with one and fulfillment with another...and he calls it love. In the new relationship his needs are being met.

## "Self-Destruct Marriage" Flesh

**Bill:** We have come to believe, after counseling many hundreds of couples, that the marriage most vulnerable to divorce is one in which either a passive flesh or a macho flesh husband is in union with a wife who comes on too strong. And the only surefire, guaranteed way to defuse such a "self-destruct" marriage is for both parties to come to the end of their flesh trips and allow Christ to express His

Life through them so they are able to meet one another's needs. Otherwise, it's typically just a matter of time until the marriage begins either to explode or implode.

**Anabel:** The wife can be so detrimental in this kind of relationship by not being sensitive to the things her husband believes are important. She is often resistant to his will, expressing a lack of confidence in his decisions, correcting him in public (even in jest it's a no-no), or through excessive correction, commonly called nagging.

Submission is a *ministry* to our husbands; when we view it that way, it becomes more palatable as opposed to being obligatory.

## Making the Right Decisions

While we're on the topic of submission, let's talk about the "decision-making" process. This seems to be an area of great discussion, or should we say great dissension? I've had some pretty difficult struggles with this, especially when I've seen Bill making decisions for the family that I strongly felt were not the right ones. It has taken time, but the Lord has made Bill far more sensitive to me in this aspect of our relationship.

**Bill:** In the figure below, the left side represents the husband and the right the wife. Remember that each one is equipped with certain talents, abilities, and spiritual gifts by the One who created them. His goal is that they learn, under His authority, how to *agape* one another by faith.

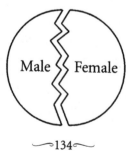

Let's create a hypothetical situation—say Anabel and I are faced with the question, "Should we plant a big garden this spring?"

Generally speaking, as a male I approach decisions from a logical perspective, whereas Anabel approaches them intuitively. I might say, "Here are my reasons for believing we should plant a big garden: A,B,C, etc." Anabel, on the other hand, might say, "Well, I just don't *feel* we should plant a garden this year." If I were to ask why, she'd be hard pressed to give me seven logical reasons why she *feels* the way she does.

For a long time I wrote off her ideas as illogical, but finally the Lord got it through my thick skull that Anabel is not illogical, she's *intuitive,* and that is excellent! She is the main source of intuitive input in our relationship, and if I ignore her, *I'm* the one who is being illogical. I'm cutting off my nose to spite my face.

God will speak to me through Anabel if I'll just listen to her. It's amazing, guys, how often you can share problems with your wife in areas that she may know little about, and God will give you solutions through her. He'll honor the fact that you humble yourself and listen.

## One in Christ, One in Success

The Lord taught me the literality of the "oneness" He designed for Christians in marriage not long after I entered the counseling ministry. I had resigned my job as a psychology professor in Oklahoma and had moved our family to Springfield, Missouri, to open a counseling office. For many weeks, my appointment calendar was clean as a whistle. It was tough; one pay period I got fifty-nine American dollars. During these lean months, I began to sense that God wanted Anabel to begin a women's Bible study, and she agreed.

We put a small ad in the paper inviting women to come to our home the following Thursday morning, and forty-seven showed up! Our house wouldn't hold that crowd, so they moved to a larger house. The next week, as I recall, seventy-five came. The larger house wouldn't hold that many women, so a hall was rented and one hundred and twenty attended!

The following Saturday, I was washing dishes (loving Anabel) and talking to the Lord. "Lord…I don't understand all this. Anabel has her hundreds and I can't even get 'em to come to me one at a time! I'm the one You sent to save Springfield from their sins, not Anabel! I'm not trying to get smart with You, Sir. I'm a broken man, and if You want me to be in a tiny ministry, that's just fine. I don't need the big crowd, but I sure would appreciate it if You'd explain what is happening."

Thoughts began to come to mind, and by faith, I believe that they were the Lord's response to me. "Bill, you really admire Anabel, don't you?"

I said, "Yessir, I do. She's a very competent person."

He said, "Tell Me, Bill, aren't you and Anabel one?"

"Yessir."

"And you've always wanted to be a walking Bible concordance, like she is, haven't you?"

I said, "Yessir, I have."

"Well, congratulations. Now you are."

*Do you see what He told me?!* God said that jagged line in Figure 4.2 doesn't exist. Anabel and I are like a cue ball on a snooker table. We are one! You say, "Oh, Bill, you're taking that too literally; it's just that God *sees* you as one." Okay. I'll buy that. Now since God makes up the rules and He sees us as one, what are we? One! That means I'm free! I don't *have to compete* with this hard-charger anymore! Whatever she can do, *I* am doing; whatever I can do, she's doing. We are one. We don't compete or envy one another any more than an elbow envies a wrist! This is a choice, not a feeling. We're in this thing together!

## Talking and Listening

So let's apply this oneness to the decision-making process. Anabel and I have discussed the pros and cons of a garden. She's told me what she thinks and I've listened to her. When she was talking, I gave her eye contact, and I wasn't leafing through the pages of the seed catalog, saying "Yeah, I'm listening. Go ahead with whatever it was you wanted to say." We've both prayed about it, and finally I've said to her, "Well, I'd like to go ahead with the garden."

Now what I don't need her to say is, "That's strange; I prayed about it too, and that certainly isn't the answer that I received from the Lord."

That would eat my lunch. It would really devastate me, and would make it more difficult for me to let Christ live through me in the situation.

## Defusing a Potential Bomb

**Anabel:** At this point, Bill needs me to encourage him, to support him and to reassure him. I might say, "All right, what shall we plant? If we can decide now, I'll run down to the hardware store and get the seeds this afternoon."

**Bill:** Naturally, that kind of encouragement would make me feel good. But three months later, after one of the biggest droughts in the history of Texas, we're sitting at the breakfast table and the man on the radio says, "Well folks, it looks like another hot, dry week coming up." Let's say the boys are still young, and all six of us are at the table. What do I not need from my wife?

**Anabel:** I could be very overt and cruel and say something deliberately designed to make you look bad in front of the boys; "Have you been out to see the garden lately, guys? We've labeled it 'Gillham's Folly.' One of these days your dad will learn to listen to me—but oh, no! He had to have *his* garden. With the money we've spent on that little project, I could have gone to the grocery store and bought fresh vegetables for the next two years!"

Or I could be very covert: "What did the weatherman say today? I...uh...didn't hear it."

**Bill:** If Anabel were to say something like that, you can bet that sin would speak to me with an Okie accent, in first person pronouns, trying to get me to react to her assault on my credibility.

Through my macho flesh, sin will give me thought responses like, "Shut up! I told you to shut up about that garden, and now I'm telling you for the last time!" I'd be seething with feelings of hatred and revenge because my wife had emasculated me in front of my sons.

But if I had passive flesh, sin would put thoughts into my mind like this, "Why? *Why* did I ever mention planting a garden? Oh Lord, if You'll ever let this pass away and be forgotten, I'll be so grateful to You. When will I learn that I *never* have good ideas, that she's *always* right? Oh, if only I were different, but I'll never change." After whining for a few minutes, I'd fade to black.

That passivity is flesh, not spirit, just as surely as dominance is flesh. It is developed from day one, since infancy. The passive-flesh person has sought the goals of human acceptance and getting his needs for security and comfort satisfied through *weakness* in much the same manner as a puppy tucks its tail and rolls over on its back.

Sin controls the passive person with either self-justifying or self-abasing thoughts; that is, any thoughts which will justify his staying away from where the action is, or where personal accountability is essential.

## What About the Children?

**Anabel:** Just what might take place within the boys if Bill had macho-flesh outbursts? One son might be thinking, "Give it to her Dad. No woman is ever going to talk to me that way!" And even though he "agrees" with what his dad is doing, his emotions run rampant with hostility or anger. He carries this to school with him and pours his venom out on the girls or becomes involved with other boys who are hostile and angry. He begins to be programmed just like his dad.

But how about another son who has a very sensitive personality? He might get sick at his stomach and ask to be excused from the table. He goes to his room, closes the door and sits on the bed and cries. His emotions are running rampant, too. He feels insecure and hates the scenes that his dad and mom play. And he hates himself. He's "too old to cry" and he begins to have such thoughts as these: "I'll *never* get married! What's wrong with me? I hate myself. I wish I were dead! If only Mom and Dad knew what they're doing to me. I hate being here at home. I just wish I didn't have to ever come home again." He isn't too excited about family vacations or going to the movies together. He knows what's going to happen and so he spends a lot of time alone, or finds another kid who "feels" like he does.

And "the iniquity of fathers (and mothers) are visited on the children and the grandchildren to the third and fourth generations" (Exodus 34:7c). That isn't an angry God. That is the result of parents who hold tenaciously to their flesh, refusing to allow Christ to live through them, and in so doing, pass on to their children the patterns that have plagued them all their lives.

What might be happening to our sons if Bill responded

with passive-flesh. The stronger one might think something like this, "Boy! I'll punch my wife out if she ever smarts off like that! I'd like to see Dad flatten Mom just once." That son would lose respect for his father, and would feed the fire of woman-hating.

The more sensitive son would probably react in much the same way as he did when Dad used the macho technique.

## Christ, the Great "Bomb Defuser"

**Bill:** That's a graphic description of what I don't need from my wife. What do I need to hear from you, Anabel, when the forecaster gives his more-hot-dry-weather report on the radio.

**Anabel:** You need me to say something like, "Now don't worry about our garden, Bill. Everyone's garden has burned to a crisp. We did what we thought was right. We prayed about it. For goodness sake, just forget it now. We'll try again next year."

## Love on a Silver Platter

**Bill:** Do you notice those pronouns in her statement to me? *Our...we...we'll...?* When my wife treats me that way, I pray, "Oh, thank You, Lord, for such a woman. You know how I blew that garden deal, but this dear woman has saved my bacon in front of my sons!" This response from Anabel fills me with love for her, so much so that I just want to carry her around on a silver platter.

**Anabel:** Isn't that what every wife wants? She longs to be treasured by her husband.

**Bill:** But I want to say something in all kindness. Your husband will never be able to carry you around on that silver platter until you choose to get on the plate and stay there.

**Anabel:** We must always remember that a woman is never in an inferior position when she is in the place God created for her.

# SEXUAL ONENESS BEYOND THE BEDROOM

*Your husband needs to believe that you chose him out of all the men in the world to be just yours, and that you think he is very masculine, very strong, very capable, and you love him more than ever.*

# Chapter Nine

**B**ill: We heard this story years ago—neither of us recall the source. But it illustrates the different ways men and women view the physical relationship. The story is about a young couple, very committed to the Lord, who are engaged to be married.

## Two More Weeks of Frustration

It's past midnight, and they've been to a movie. He has tenderly kissed her goodnight two or three times, and he's heading down the front walk to his car. The young man is praying, "Oh Lord, I want to thank You for giving me the strength to keep my physical desires under control all during our dating. You know it hasn't been easy!

"Lord, there are still two more weeks till we get married, and that means two more weeks that I'll have to restrain myself. I know Your grace is sufficient, but if You could just let these two weeks zip by I'd certainly be grateful!"

We're talking about a frustrated young man. On a one-to-ten scale, his fulfillment level is about at four.

## Two Precious Weeks to Savor

Now let's look in on the bride-to-be. She's standing inside the house with her back against the door, his kisses still warm on her lips, an enraptured look on her face. They had eaten popcorn out of the same sack at the movies, and to her, this was such an intimate, special experience that she slipped one of the kernels into the pocket of her sweater so she could press it in her diary. She has taken it from her pocket and is holding it close to her lips.

She's praying, too: "Oh Lord, what a marvelous, glorious evening! What bliss! (She kisses the kernel of popcorn tenderly.) In two wonderful weeks we'll be married! These are going to be the most glorious two weeks of my life!

"Lord, let me savor every wedding shower. Let me linger over every gift. Let me live each lovely experience to the fullest, so that I will be able to remember every precious moment."

You can see that her fulfillment level is registering at about an eight or maybe even a nine.

## Living in Two Different Worlds

When the two weeks pass, the guy finally gets his princess into the castle and raises the drawbridge. His attitude is: "All right, Let's get on with this thing! Rain on that popcorn routine!" And he muffs it eighteen ways from Sunday!

Guys, we have got to get it through our thick heads that, when it comes to women, we're dealing with "popcorn-type people." It's not uncommon to discover in counseling sessions that if the husband feels he has an exciting sex life, he also believes he has a pretty good marriage. He might rate his marriage about a seven or an eight, and he's shocked to discover that his wife is rating it about a two because she views marriage as far more than a sexual relationship. If she is not getting her TLC needs met, her desire for sexual intimacy will be one of the first things to diminish.

It's rare to discover a case where sex is holding the marriage together. I could count on one hand the number of couples I've counseled who stated that they both felt they had a great sex life but that everything else was out of sync.

**Anabel:** Our popcorn story only begins to illustrate the difference in the sexual makeup of men and women. In actual fact, the difference is so immense that it's difficult to define. The sex act, for the woman, is the ultimate in giving and expressing love. Unfortunately, many women today enter into this intimate relationship outside of marriage, simply to keep from losing a particular man's companionship. But any woman would confess that it is only when the man is "her special man" that the sex act is the most fulfilling to her.

Sex for the woman begins at 6:00 a.m. She notices the way her husband says, "Good morning," and is nurtured through his tenderness, attentiveness, and kindness throughout the day. This creates the desire within her to express her love for him, and she will respond to his sexual advances.

**Bill:** On the other hand, the male can have a horrible day at work, receive no love notes or tenderness of any kind, and then see a curvy female on the way home and be ready for passionate love the moment he steps through the door. We don't mean to imply that sex isn't pleasurable to females, but the two genders certainly differ in their views.

In one of his lectures, author Josh McDowell cites a survey that makes the point very clear. He asked Christian singles who had engaged in premarital sex to write down the reason they had done so.

The males responded, "I needed *it*."

The females stated, "I loved *him*." Consider the implications of that.

## Unhappy Sexual Beginnings

**Anabel:** I doubt there is one woman reading this book who is totally free from some negative aspect of sexual intimacy. Sex has been degraded to such a level of vulgar exploitation and public display that we have to fight to keep this act holy in front of our children. It's difficult for us to remember that God created sexual intercourse, that God views this act when it takes place, and that, within the marriage relationship, it is holy before Him.

**Bill:** Sometimes those negative aspects of sexuality begin for a woman early in life. A little girl learns about herself from the feedback she gets from others, and her mother is her primary female role model. If Mom sends out rejection vibes to the little girl, then she will not be able to relate to females. She learns, "*I'm* not a feminine person. Let's face it, some girls are and some aren't, and I am not. Oh, how I wish I were different."

Much later the girl discovers that by dispensing sexual favors to boys she is able to attract them. This "proves" to her that she *is* feminine. So she goes overboard. She may even become sexually aggressive to the point of seducing males.

## Is She a Nymphomaniac?

Do you know what we've discovered in counseling these dear, hurting women? They rarely, if ever, reach a sexual climax. Tell me, is it sex they're after? Are they the kind of sex maniacs Hollywood would have us believe they are? No. They are trying to "prove" they are feminine in order to accept themselves as female. Her feeler is stuck.

So we're back to the same dynamic again: People need to be able to accept (love) themselves, and not understanding that their acceptance must be anchored in Christ, they use all sorts of do-it-yourself projects in order to achieve that acceptance.

On the other hand, the woman who was rejected by her dad in childhood will often be sexually promiscuous in order to acquire male acceptance. She is willing to trade sexual favors for three hours of TLC from a male. She too, rarely, if ever, reaches a sexual climax. We can readily see that it isn't the sex she seeks, but the love, the male acceptance she's been deprived of. Again, the stuck feeler is in control.

Should this woman get saved, learning to rest in God's total acceptance will bring freedom from much of her intense drive for male acceptance. Each of these women, in order to appropriate a positive, new self-image, must agree with God's Word that she has died as to who she was, and that she is now re-created as a new woman in Christ—that she is a "new civilian" and no longer has to heed "Sgt. Sin's" commands. This will enable her to build an entirely new, healthy, biblical self-esteem.

## Victims of Sexual Abuse

**Anabel:** While we're talking about negative aspects of sex, we must remember those men and women who have been sexually abused. Being a victim of sexual abuse creates special problems because of the total involvement of the person. Results can range from fear of sex to feeling "dirty"; from hate and bitterness for the person involved to hate and bitterness toward oneself; from sexual promiscuity to impotency; from homosexuality to frigidity; from anger to guilt. These reactions can span the whole field of negative emotions.

Here's an analogy: Let's say that you are ten years old. You're out in the woods on a family outing, and you've wandered off by yourself. You hear a noise, turn, and see a bear cub digging for some ants. You creep closer to watch. Suddenly, the mother bear thunders out of a thicket! She surmises you're up to no good, so she attacks. She mauls you and leaves you a mass of blood and tears. That happens to you one time. Just once.

What is going to happen to you every time you see a bear—even a "Gentle Ben"? Are you kidding? You *know* about bears. You've encountered one, and your emotions are "stuck" as far as bears or anything to do with bears is concerned. The minute you see a bear, you become emotionally incapacitated! Your emotional tolerance for a bear is less than one point on a one-to-ten scale because your feeler is stuck on a throbbing ten where bears are involved!

You can allow this experience to keep you from ever "going into the woods" again, from ever going to the San Diego Zoo, or from even reading "The Three Bears" to your children.

Now apply that story to having been sexually abused. Your emotions are stuck on a nine or so and any sexual stimulus causes you such emotional discomfort that you want no part of it.

## Set Free from the Past—In Christ

**Bill:**  Anabel and I have learned through counseling that those who have suffered sexual abuse can experience

Christ overcoming its debilitating effects. This happens as they identify with Him through His death, burial, and resurrection. There will still be a struggle; the Deceiver doesn't give up easily, but Christ-in-you will overcome.

If the battle rages intensely, I would suggest you overtly rebuke and bind the Deceiver and his legions for the fear they have instilled in you and offer yourself to the Holy Spirit to be filled with the peace of Jesus Christ.

By learning how to relax in Him, you can begin to be set free from the past no matter now intensely you have been abused. You have been buried, raised, and made alive with Christ and you are totally forgiven of all the sins you may have committed as you sought to deal with your problem. Moreover, Christ is now your very Life, living within you to live through you. He's scrubbed you clean! He says, "What I have called clean, don't you call unclean!" (Colossians 2:12-13, 3:3-4; Acts 10:15). The Holy Spirit says to the loose-living Corinthians, "I betrothed you to one husband, that to Christ I might present you a pure virgin" (2 Corinthians 11:2). You are a "pure virgin" again in God's opinion. View this as rows of black print on white paper and you'll remain in bondage to your stuck feeler. View it as reality and your mental chains will be broken!

## Sex as a Means of Manipulation

**Anabel:** It is quite common for women to use sex to control or manipulate. Too many of us have the attitude: If you have been very good, Husband, I will reward you tonight, and we will make love. If you have not performed to suit me (meaning that you have not sufficiently met my needs), I may develop a severe headache before I go to bed, complain about my back hurting or how tired I am. That is not Christ living through me. You see, Christ does not cease to be my Life when I walk into my bedroom. He is my Life, period.

## A Special Time for Prayer

**Bill:** Our thinking has been polluted in the world, and we have believed the lie that we must hang the Holy Spirit on the hook in the hall as we walk through the bedroom door. It is not only appropriate, but incumbent upon me to pray, prior to entering into the sex act, "Lord, I'm trusting You to express tenderness and love through me to my wife. Use me to make this a very special, enjoyable time for her." Hey, if we pray for mundane things like parking places, does it make sense to enter into something as significant as the sex act in our own strength?

I have counseled men who are troubled with premature ejaculation, impotency, and other sexual performance problems (not physical in origin) who have experienced significant improvement through trusting Christ as Life during the sex act with their wife. Reading the books we're going to recommend is most helpful. But allowing Christ's Life to be expressed through you remains the key to being able to do what the books teach.

Now, we're certainly not teaching that Christ is having sex with the spouse, for heaven's sake. I am the vessel; He is the Life of the vessel. In my shop I have an electric sander. The electricity does not sand the boards; it is simply the life of the sander. The sander sands the board. The electricity enables the sander to perform as it was intended to by its creator.

## A New Creation, A New Mind-Set

And remember, this isn't a "power-of-positive-thinking" type approach to living victoriously in your Christian walk. And it's not a gimmick to help you off the launch pad till you are strong enough to fly solo! This is normal Christianity till you eject from your earthsuit.

As we said in Chapter One, this is the gospel. It's reality, man! Every Christian is a new creation in Christ Jesus:

> *Therefore if any man is in Christ, he **is** a new creature; the old things **passed** away; behold, new things **have** come* (2 Corinthians 5:17).

**Anabel:** What Bill has said to the men about having the right mind-set is true for women, too. "Lord, use me to make this all that my husband needs it to be." Setting our minds on His Life within us gives us the power we need to enter into sexual intimacy with our hubbys, even when that might be the last thing on earth we want to do at the time.

Many women will concur that there have been times when they have willingly responded to their husband's sexual overtures even though they themselves did not reach a climax. Their attitude during those times had been one of comfort at having pleased their husbands.

## Lies About Sexuality

**Bill:** The message from the world via TV, movies, print, books, and magazines is that unless a husband is able to produce surefire ecstasy for his wife each time they go to bed, he's not a "real" man. That's a lie. Those scripts are written by hot-blooded individuals with vivid imaginations. Watching, listening to, or reading their lies sets people up for frustration. Let's face it, it's impossible for any human to keep on bettering his last performance indefinitely in any endeavor on Planet Earth. This includes the sex act.

Similarly, the world tells us that unless a wife is a tiger in bed, she is a failure as a sex partner. Another lie. The unspoken conclusion is that the husband is justified in searching for greener pastures outside his marriage vow. That, too, is a lie.

## Broken Rules Produce Unhealthy Memories

Remember, God's laws are for our supreme well-being. He is not a party-pooper because he limits us to sex with our spouses. That's for our best good! I wish you could hear some of the stories I've heard from both men and women who have violated this one law of God and are now struggling with the memories.

I remember a businessman who came to see me who felt that his wife was not an exciting sex partner. His secretary started inviting him over to her place, teasing him with suggestions about favors she'd do for him. He eventually fell for it, and sure enough, she was more exciting than his wife. (Bear in mind that the secretary had a hidden agenda; she wanted to become the guy's new wife. So she, no doubt, was trying her best to show him what he had been "missing" in life.)

After those encounters, the man had something to compare his wife with, and the comparison wasn't in her favor. To this day, he would give anything not to have fallen into Satan's trap in that one critical area. Sin regularly serves up the memories to him. He would have been so much happier if he had stayed out of that "greener pasture."

## Four Keys to Successful Feminine Sexuality

**Anabel:** Of course, wives have a responsibility to keep sexual attraction alive in their marriages. Physically, the wife should be

- Appealing
- Available

- Agreeable
- Aggressive (at times)

**Appealing...** God fashioned the male to respond to a visual stimulus. This is not being a "dirty-minded" man. It's normal. (Why do you suppose the Dallas Cowboys cheerleaders are hired? To lead cheers?) The wife should recognize this and take care of herself physically. She should be appealing to her husband. She should dress for him, wear her hair the way he likes it, smell good, and watch her weight. Most husbands work around women all day who look good and smell good. It's that simple.

**Available...** not always working until you're dog-tired when you go to bed and are not interested—even a little bit—in love-making. Too tired. It means planning your time so that your husband won't get the idea that he's on your list of things to do. Too busy. Being available means you are saying, "I meant it when I signed up for this job— and I'm ready to carry out my part of the contract."

**Agreeable...** humor some of his romantic plans. (They do every so often have romantic plans. But I readily confess that the wife is usually the "romantic planner"—and that's all right. Don't be resentful. Just take the reins and go for it.)

**Aggressive...** it means just that! Every so often plan a romantic tete-a-tete, and you take the lead. Get a tempting gown, plan a rubdown, get in the Jacuzzi with him. Be creative!

## Bad Habits that Damage Good Sex

**Bill:** Those things are important to me, and I'm sure every other husband will dog-ear this portion of the book. If she isn't on her toes, a wife can really damage the physical relationship, by...

- Being slovenly or lazy
- Being undisciplined and disorganized
- Being careless with money
- Being careless about her physical appearance
- Being sexually incompatible with her husband
- Being a nagging, demanding, dictating woman

Any one of these things can cause him to react adversely, especially in the physical area of the relationship. Many women don't understand that the sex act is more than a physical need for the husband—it's a major emotional release, too. And if you, his wife, are the cause of this emotional pressure (i.e., by doing some of the things listed above), he will be tempted to find that emotional release somewhere else. Incidently, the things we've listed here apply to the husband as well.

## What Turns Him On?

**Anabel:** It's difficult, but I have to somehow accept the fact that my husband may come home from work and need sex because he saw a voluptuous female walking down the street, or because one of the secretaries at work dressed seductively on that particular day. (Praise God, he comes home!)

He may also come home needing sex—intensely—because his boss chewed him out at work. Or because the project that he has been researching for ten months resulted in complete failure. Or because the man at the desk next to him got promoted. Or because he sees me in the same dress that I have been wearing for the last year and his paycheck just won't allow me to buy a new one.

What does your husband need? He needs you, his wife, to assure him that he is still "the greatest." He needs to believe that you chose him out of all the men in the world to be just yours, and that you think he is very masculine, very strong, very capable, and you love him more than ever.

## Is Love Spelled S-E-X?

**Bill:** Sometimes a desperate wife asks, "What do I do with a husband who has an industrial-strength sex drive?" I've counseled guys who want sex with their wives three times a day at age forty! Are their wives supposed to dedicate the entire day to being a sex partner? Is this God's will for them? Are some males just born this way? Is there no hope? I mean, a woman can't even catch the evening news living with a guy like that.

Invariably, I find that the Christian man with a Tarzan-size sex appetite was rejected by his folks. Here's a typical case from my files: This man was a star athlete in high school. He had been named the outstanding running back in one of America's major metro centers. Guess how many games his folks attended. Zero! From that one fact you can probably guess the rest of his story. His parents never spent any time with him. He felt lonely. He felt rejected. He felt he wasn't worth their time. He felt unloved.

He got into sex his sophomore year of high school. It was the first "love" experience he'd ever had, and it blew him away. He promptly went overboard and began seducing every girl possible. You see, his sexual fulfillment was being bonded to his intensified need for love. This was the result of a lifetime of parental deprivation. He quickly learned to spell "love": S-E-X.

Ultimately, the young man got saved and eventually married. However, he forced his wife to be the source of his love supply instead of looking to Christ as his Source. And he almost wore the poor woman out. The guy needed love, but he didn't know of any other way to get it. He had experienced no love other than sexual love. He needed to understand his true identity in Christ, to comprehend His total love and acceptance. He needed to understand that although Christ's love is not always *felt*, it is always to be *believed*. And, by being believed, it becomes *known*.

The man appropriated his true identity in Christ. He rejected Sin's first-person, singular pronoun onslaught. And by thus learning how to enter into "God's rest," he began to relax in his total acceptance in Christ. The Bible began to come alive to him, reinforcing His new identity, and eventually his sex drive began to modify.

(His wife was amazed at how the anchorman on the evening news had aged over the years.)

### Dressed for the Occasion

**Anabel:** It bears repeating: God created sex, and He intends for married couples to experience pleasure in that aspect of His creation. He views this act, and it is holy before Him. Keeping this in mind will allow us to enter into the act of marriage with fewer inhibitions.

I admire the preacher's wife who confided what she had given her husband for his birthday. She went to the lingerie department and chose a very risqué nightie, then to the gift wrap department and had it wrapped in masculine paper. (Raised a few eyebrows in that department.) When she presented her gift to her hubby, he said that it was one of the most appreciated gifts he had ever received.

Our husbands don't want us to be the aggressors in our sexual relationship all the time, but they really love it when we occasionally surprise them.

**Bill:** Some men would be *very surprised* if something like that were to happen! I remember a husband who complained that his wife (a very attractive lady) wore granny gowns to bed and slept with her hair in curlers. He asked her to wear see-through nighties in the privacy of their bedroom. The wife refused, stating that she saw no purpose in such a request. She said it made her feel uncomfortable to be half-dressed and that she refused to lower herself to such common behavior. One day I noticed her jogging through the neighborhood in flimsy nylon briefs. Apparently she looked better jogging (for all the neighbor men to ogle) than she did for her husband in their own bedroom.

Yes, a husband is delighted when his wife adds a spicy surprise to their sex life. I want to add, however, that sometimes a husband makes sexual demands on his wife which he might view as innovative and exciting, but which are offensive to her. If he insists that she comply with his demands, it is not Christ expressing His Life through the husband. Christ would ever impose His will just to get his needs satisfied. That's a flesh trip.

## Doing Your Homework

**Anabel:** I'd like to suggest that if your sex-life isn't all that it should be, try educating yourself. Look at it this way—when you first married and found out that apple pie was your hubby's very favorite, you wanted to please him so you started trying recipes. Finally the day came when, after your numerous attempts at getting it just right, you put a piece of pie in front of him, he tasted it and said, "This is it! Just like Momma used to make!"

Well, perfecting the sex act is much more important than baking an apple pie "just like Mother used to make." There are many good books on the subject, but we recommend *Love Life* and *Intended for Pleasure*, by Dr. Ed Wheat. We think it's worth doing your homework, because the sex act binds us together uniquely in our marriage. This is the one way in which we are able to completely express our love for each other—body, soul and spirit.

# TO BE TRULY FEMININE

*The godly women in Scripture reveal
that a female is worthy simply because
of who she is. She is indispensable because
God's work is able to come to fruition
in and through her.*

# ─ Chapter Ten ─

*Hmm…they've all got partners except for Adam.*
*So let's create a female human being corresponding*
*to him. Only let's not start from scratch with her;*
*let's create her from his rib. There. That's a*
*creative twist! This way they'll both understand that*
*she is part of him, and though equal to him, she,*
*too, will have her unique role in Our scheme of things.*
*Boy, it's going to be fun to see the look on his face*
*when We wake him up*
(Adapted from Genesis 2:18-24).

**Anabel:** Just as a man's view of himself affects his relationship with his wife, the same is true of a woman. If a wife is not in touch with her true, God-given femininity, she will experience many conflicts in her marriage. She will find herself competing with her husband, refusing to listen, attempting to usurp his rightful role as head of the household. Or she will be so intimidated by him that she cannot express herself. She will be motivated by fear, not by godly respect. In either case, she will not be her true self in the marriage relationship.

We hear a lot of talk about women these days—their rights, their proper roles and their emotional needs. What does it mean, before God, to be truly feminine?

## A Super-Duper Tomboy

One of the most tender and intimate moments I remember with my dad occurred while we were sitting out on the back porch steps one evening. I was sitting between his knees, and he had his arms around my neck. My mother had just undergone a hysterectomy. I didn't understand Dad's poignant words when he said to me, "You know, Honey, you're the only little boy I'll ever have."

I don't know whether it was because I wanted to please my dad or not, but I was already a super-duper tomboy. The neighborhood kids often gathered in our backyard, and there were several boys in the group. That didn't matter to me. If we played Cowboys and Indians, I was the chief. If we played cops and robbers, I was the head honcho—be it the sheriff or the "godfather." I even remember Dad tying ropes in the mulberry tree so I could be Tarzan.

In the "races down under the hill" during recess in the sixth grade, I always won. I reveled in defeating Joe Harold—he was my boyfriend.

Another "red letter" day was the annual trek up Cavanaugh Mountain. I had a crush on Robert Henry Kendrick. How was I going to get him to notice me? The same way I had been getting boys to notice me ever since the backyard get-togethers. I did whatever he did better than he could do it!

Robert Henry was very definitely the leader of the pack, but I was right by his side all the way up to the top of the mountain. I can still remember the thrill of sitting with him on the big flat rock looking out over the Poteau River Valley, waiting for the others to catch up with us.

He said something to the effect of, "You're quite a mountain climber." He'd noticed me! My heart fairly sang, but my joy was short-lived. He carried another girl down the mountain because she had a blister on her foot.

Was I starting to get the picture?

## Maybe Being a Girl Is Allright

About this time, I became aware of something else—Humphrey Bogart and Lauren Bacall. That was nice, and so was the movie *Mrs. Miniver* with Greer Garson and Walter Pidgeon. I liked what I saw. Two people—married—who had fun together, who respected each other as individuals and who loved each other deeply. I began to think, *maybe being a girl isn't all that bad.*

Some people would call that "cultural conditioning." I call it "Creationist conception." I was beginning to see what God had created me to be...something very beautiful...something very special...a female.

We've discussed the male's needs and read about what true masculinity involves. Now what about femininity? What does it mean to be truly feminine?

**Bill:** If we asked a group of women that question, many of their answers would reflect the culture of the day. They would mention career goals, their style of dress, their physical appearance, or some other understanding of personal fulfillment. The answers might have been quite different if they had come from another continent, or a group of women in 1900, or in the Middle Ages, or during the time of Christ.

It is imperative that women have a standard—an immutable standard—if they want to discover the true meaning of femininity.

## Feminine = Completing

**Anabel:** The source of the word feminine is derived from the female, and the female was created by God. He said, *It isn't good for the man to be alone. I will make him a helper corresponding to* (Lit.) *him* (Genesis 2:18).

Our understanding of "femininity" will emerge as we accept the impeccable integrity of God. He designed the female to complement or complete the male in marriage. Let me hasten to say right now that the single woman is *not* incomplete. We are "complete in Him" (Colossians 2:10). That "completeness" will never be removed. It is part of the finished work of Christ.

But when I go to God...volitionally...and announce to Him that I want to be a wife, one of the duties He assigns to me is to complement/complete the husband. I choose to step into that role and I choose to accept that assignment as part of the marriage covenant. But marriage cannot be the prerequisite for being complete, nor is it the prerequisite for being feminine.

Let's look first at the meaning of femininity in the marriage relationship. As man and wife (and Adam and Eve were man and wife), we complete each other *in the marriage relationship* as God intended. Once we discover how the male is to be completed, then we can fulfill our feminine role in marriage by meeting the male needs. How do I, as a woman, complete the male? It certainly involves a great deal more than sexual completion.

Consider the male's ability to gather data in a certain

situation. Generally speaking, he is very logical, but he is not very intuitive. We females are intuitive, so as we share our perspectives with him via our God-endowed intuition, we add that dimension to complement his logic.

Bill: In interpersonal relationships, males are typically not as "people oriented" as women. Men are not emotionally designed by the Creator the way women are. The woman adds to the oneness equation a depth of communication and sensitivity. A wise husband who is humble before his Creator is grateful for God's gift of a wife and he willingly receives her along with the attributes which he lacks by the Creator's design.

Anabel: It will be helpful to our understanding of the female if we review the needs of the male from a feminine perspective. Please read this entire section with an open heart before the Lord. It may not be politically correct, but I trust you will find it biblically correct. A man needs praise from his wife. The female, being created to "help," is to complete that need; she should allow the male to perform for her. In doing so, *the woman is able to praise him.* That's part of being feminine. Should I consistently send signals to my husband that I don't need his help or refuse to praise him, I fail to meet that need God gave to him and I am negating my femininity. I am rebelling against the Lord God's plan.

The male requires headship. Being created as a "helper" to meet that need, *the woman allows the male to operate as the head.* This is part of my ministry to my husband. I must view this as unto the Lord. That's being feminine. If I compete with the male for the authority role (be it my husband, my boss, or the meterman) by being domineering, aggressive and demanding, then I am competing, not "completing." I am denying my feminine make-up.

Like praise and headship, God gave the male a need for

a physical relationship. This need is to be met within the bounds of God's plan; He created us and He knows what is best for His creation. Meeting this need is reserved for the marriage relationship. As *the woman completes her husband physically*, she is being feminine.

Rearing children is a unique feminine trait. That's also part of being female. Woman was created physiologically to bear children. She has been given certain emotional qualities and certain intellectual qualities that are unique to her as a female, designed for the specific purpose of rearing children. Yes, childrearing is definitely a part of the female role God lovingly bestowed upon woman.

## More than a Man's Woman

But, if completing the male and bearing and rearing children were all that I was created for as a woman, many women would be destined for unfulfilled lives. Do you think God is unaware of the desires and the needs of the single woman? Is she less than feminine because she's single? No. She may feel she is, but that doesn't make it so. There are many Christian singles who delight in their "singleness." That's good.

Do you ever wonder if the Lord knows the depth of despair that clouds the heart of the widow? Or the cry of the woman who longs to be married? To be needed—and yet to have no one who needs me. To have been given the innate desire to build a nest—and not have anyone to 'feather the nest' for.

**Bill:** Never doubt that God knows the intensity of loneliness or the depth to which "yearning" reaches. Oh, yes. He knows. And He gave us answers long before we asked our questions. He has shown us, through His Word, that woman is able to be much more than simply a counterpart for man.

Through women in the Bible, God has demonstrated that a woman's worth extends far beyond her relationships with males, her occupation, her status, or her accomplishments in the world system. The godly women in Scripture reveal that a female is worthy simply because of who she is. She is indispensable because God's work is able to come to fruition in and through her. God's women can stand alone.

## Femininity—Role Models from Scripture

**Anabel:** Dorcas "abounded with deeds of kindness and charity" (Acts 9). She was a compassionate woman who met the needs of those around her.

Ruth's tenderness toward her bereaved mother-in-law was a declaration of true love and faithfulness. She respected Naomi and honored her wisdom.

Lydia was a businesswoman who sold "purple goods" (Acts 16). She opened her home to the early followers of the Way and was a dedicated disciple.

Esther possessed great courage and discernment; it was her wisdom and boldness that saved the Jewish nation.

Mary, Martha's sister, was a woman of deep devotion. She took her costly perfume and bathed the feet of Jesus. Perhaps someone (like her sister, maybe) said, "Oh Mary, how foolish. How insignificant...as though He would notice." But He did. Her simple act of love for the Lord has been recorded so that we might realize how He desires our overt adoration (John 12:3).

Deborah was a judge of Israel...a national leader (Judges 4 & 5). She was strong and courageous.

Mary, the mother of Jesus, was a woman of great faith and obedience (Luke 2).

The Proverbs 31 wife was a well-organized and competent wife and businesswoman.

Rahab the harlot proved herself to be trustworthy and brave (Joshua 2 and 6).

All this is feminine? Resoundingly, yes! I have listed as many different "job descriptions" as I have women. You cannot define femininity as something a woman *does*. It must be defined as something a woman *is*.

## Femininity Gone Wrong

**Bill:** Every little girl comes into her world with the God-given need to be feminine, and all females are created equal as far as these innate needs are concerned. However, each little girl's self-image as a female is molded by the people in her own unique world.

Remember, because children are self-centered, they do not learn about other people in their world. Instead, they learn about themselves as people interact with them, touch them, communicate with them, and care for them. Because of this intrinsic self-centeredness, a little girl begins to learn about herself and her femininity from the moment she draws her first breath.

**Anabel:** If she could express her need, she might ask, "Why do I feel this way, Mother? Why did that make me cry? Why is my body different? Mother, teach me how to be feminine. What does 'feminine' mean? Why am I special? How should I act?"

**Bill:** And if the child's mother does not heed her daughter's silent questions, the little girl will not learn positive things about herself. Instead, Satan will see to it that the opposite will happen—she will come to doubt her femininity. The craving for identity lying deep within her will grow as she grows, but not necessarily into the kind of beauty God intended. It may deform and intensify until it is completely out of proportion and will eventually control her. She may grow up to become...

- Sexually promiscuous
- Frigid
- Fearful
- Homosexual
- A man hater
- A woman hater
- Insecure
- Deprived of love
- Perverted
- Introverted
- Extroverted
- Self-hating

The list goes on and on describing the young woman who was never physically loved by her mother, whose mother never hugged her or kissed her or said to her, "I love you"; who never taught her feminine tasks or whispered choice feminine secrets; who never affirmed her daughter's femininity.

## Daddy's Little Girl

**Anabel:** And then there's Dad. Every little girl longs for his attention: "Carry me, Daddy. Let me go with you, Daddy. Can I hold your hand? Tell me, how do I talk to boys? Will other men be as much fun as you are? Will I find someone just like you? You make me feel so special. Thank you, Daddy, for the talk last night."

"I love you, Honey."

"Yes, I know you love me, Dad."

What a beautiful blessing a father's affection is. And if a girl is deprived of it, she searches with an almost insatiable craving all through her life for "Daddy's love"...to be held...to be touched...to be cherished...to be feminine.

## Jesus, Lover of Your Soul

Mothers fail. Fathers fail. The damage done may be minimal. Or it may be devastating.

But beyond all else, there is Father God. God created the female and God can re-create the female as He tenderly fashioned her that day in the garden.

It isn't that you have been maimed and deformed beyond recognition, beyond hope. Perhaps you are stained. Maybe you have been deceived. Most likely you have believed what people have told you—or you have suffered from what they have not told you. You have been deeply hurt by those who were supposed to love you.

Do you understand what happened when you came to Christ and said to Him, "Oh Jesus, Healer of all that is broken, please mold me and make me new"? He did just that; He took all of the unloveliness, the rejection, the broken heart, and created a new woman who is altogether lovely and totally accepted in His sight.

Would you like to be someone different, someone who doesn't have to be controlled by what she has experienced in years past? You are, my dear one! Nothing is impossible for God. Nothing is so ugly that He will turn His eyes away, so mutilated that it is beyond His ability to heal. He takes what the world has soiled and trodden under foot, and He remakes it. He takes the wounds that have been so cruelly inflicted, and cleanses them with compassionate care. He whispers words of love and encouragement, and He will never release His firm grip on your hand.

But you must ask Him to do these things. He does not force His will upon you or insist that you love Him. He patiently waits for you to accept all that He has done for you. If you want His loving touch, it is yours....

*Therefore, if any woman is in Christ Jesus, she is a beautiful new creature. All of the old things that she learned about herself that were so destructive and hurtful have passed away. Look closely…you are new!*

# TWENTY WAYS TO LOVE YOUR WIFE

*Protection. Attention. Being loved.*
*Closeness without passion. Security.*
*Safety from the "cold north winds"*
*that blow about the house. Encirclement*
*in arms that are strong. This is what*
*women are asking for, longing for,*
*praying for. Are their men listening?*

# Chapter Eleven

**A**nabel: When we began doing seminars years ago, I would ask women to finish this statement...

*"I wish my husband would love me by...."*

No matter where we went, the answers were invariably the same. In fact, we no longer ask women to answer that very important question because we already know what they are going to say. Over the years we've saved all of the replies and categorized them according to the number of times each particular answer was mentioned. We want to share the "top twenty" with you.

**Bill:** We believe that the following requests from wives

represent their longings to be loved by their husbands the same way Jesus loves His wife, the Church (Ephesians 5:25-27). Bear in mind, again, that the Greek word for love in this passage is agape, meaning *I will do the most constructive, redemptive thing I can think of for you.* The word carries the connotation of performance, not simply warm feelings. When we speak of agape, we must think of performing some act regardless of how we feel—and only Christ through you can consistently pull this off.

**Anabel:** Bill and I were presenting our seminar in a city near the ocean. It was Sunday afternoon, and you know what that means—football. Our schedule was really full, and that afternoon was going to be our only chance to explore and enjoy the beach together.

I approached the man of the house and said, "Let's go for a walk on the beach."

"I'm watching the game. The Cowboys are playing."

"But we won't have another chance. Our schedule is so full."

"I'll tell you what—why don't you go walking and I'll watch the ball game."

And I did. I readily confess that it wasn't at all like I had hoped it would be. It was more of a "regaining-my-composure" walk than the lovely, hand-in-hand stroll down the beach I had envisioned.

**Bill:** We husbands typically do not come factory equipped to hear what our wives are actually requesting. Anabel was really saying to me, "Love me today by strolling down the beach with me hand in hand." I didn't "hear" that message. But after years of growing in our marriage, as well as counseling and listening to women from all over the country, I am learning what she, and other wives are asking for…love. They don't articulate it that way. We must learn to read between the lines.

Let's begin by looking at the first of the top twenty ways.

# I Wish My Husband Would Love Me...

### #1. By Listening to Me

**Anabel:** Far and away, this has consistently been our number one reply. And, I might add, there are very few men who could have guessed what this first wish would be.

We were in Ennis, Texas, and I had just asked all of the women to finish the statement. I noticed one little lady who was probably in her late seventies. She began writing and when I picked the slips up, I dog-eared hers...I was curious. She had changed the wording a little bit and that made it even more special, but she was asking for the same simple gift that hundreds of other women have asked for: "I wish my husband *would have loved me* by listening to me." No matter how long we live, we women never outgrow this desire and it's incredibly important to us.

**Bill:** Anabel and I have asked several groups of married couples this question: "What one thing has hindered your marriage from becoming all you'd like it to be?" Thirty-nine out of every one hundred couples polled said that *communication* had been their downfall, their Waterloo.

Communication doesn't come easily. It takes a lot of time and commitment. To make matters worse, there are very few people who like to listen. Generally speaking, the first statement the listener hears brings to his mind a comment he wants to make, and that's about as far as the two-way conversation goes. Listening is a lost art.

Communication refers to the practice of discussion, which always involves at least two people. Every one of the twenty ways to love your wife in this chapter involves "communication" in one form or another. We communicate through verbal interaction, of course, but we also communicate...

- By listening, or not listening
- By touching, or not touching
- By planning, or not planning
- By participating, or not participating
- By making eye contact, or looking away
- By using body language, looks, and gestures

These little acts may seem terribly insignificant to males, but they are constantly noted by females. As you husbands read these twenty requests, I hope you will visualize what form of communication (including talking things over) will be necessary to meet your wife's needs.

### #2. By Taking My "Petty Problems" Seriously
**Anabel:** Many women remarked that their husbands often referred to their concerns as "petty problems." What are these so-called "petty problems"? They may be areas in which we are insecure and need our husbands to reassure us. They may be on-the-job dilemmas we need to discuss. They may involve an area of intuitive unrest that we "just have to talk about, please."

Here's one example:

"Honey, my car is making this funny noise." Sometimes the wife winds up feeling like an idiot because she can't explain in detail where the funny noise originates, if it has happened before, if the car is warm or cool when the noise begins, or some other technical information.

One woman told me, "When I tell my husband something like that, he looks at me as if to say, 'And just what do you want me to do about it?'"

One of the most infamous "petty problems" is the grocery budget. How well I remember when we were watching our pennies. Bill would say to me, "Honey, our money is really tight this month. Cut back on the groceries." We never cut back on anything else!

Sometimes (I graciously use that word) when a wife tries to discuss the rising cost of groceries and clothes for the children, her husband communicates, in one way or another, "That's your problem. Just stay within the budget."

Here are some more "petty problems":

"I can't figure out what my boss wants from me on this project."

"The washing machine got spots of oil on the clothes when I wash them."

"I don't know whether to include the Bakers in our dinner party or not."

"The toilet made a gurgling sound when I flushed it this morning."

**Bill:** What our wives are saying is, "I'd like for you to discuss this with me." It may be difficult for a husband to appreciate the importance of some of his wife's problems when he's been dealing with millions of dollars a day as an investor, making life and death decisions as a physician, overseeing forty-four employees as a foreman, or barely surviving in a job that he dislikes intensely. Maybe he's been talking to people all day and doesn't want to talk about any more problems. Whatever the case, he looks at his wife in disbelief, appalled that she would bother him with such mundane trivia when he has heavy things on his mind.

Every husband has to understand that his wife *needs* to talk to him, and she needs for him to show interest as he listens and that's a ten! Christ, through us, is able to accomplish this.

**Anabel:** Listening is a common courtesy. And when I ask for Bill's advice, I am placing him in his proper position as my authority...my spiritual leader. So very often, men want to be the "head of the home" because of the *power* it bestows on them. But God has placed them in that role because of the *responsibility* it gives them.

If my husband doesn't listen to me and give me his input when I need it, then he does not have the prerogative of reprimanding me if I make mistakes. Headship involves a lot more than everyone jumping when the head says "frog."

### #3. By Communicating More Openly with Me

**Bill:** A strong, silent male can cause big problems in the marriage relationship. If he uses grunts, shrugs, raised eyebrows, "uh-huh, huh-uh," and two-word phrases such as, "Who knows?"; "Who cares?"; "I'm tired."; "So what?"; and other such responses, he's not loving his wife.

Faced with this kind of inattentiveness, a woman may start chattering most of the time out of sheer frustration or talking on the phone for hours on end. She may begin to nag. Or she might just give up trying and cease all communication. Due to the husband's noncommunicative attitude, the burden for keeping the marriage alive falls totally on the wife.

There are men who seem to have the idea that their only responsibility in the marriage is to bring home the paycheck. They sometimes find out too late (after they've been served the divorce papers) that their wives could not, indeed, would not tolerate that perspective.

**Anabel:** A woman wants her man to communicate with her on an emotional level. She wants him to be willing to reveal his feelings and to become vulnerable. We call it "talking about deep things." A female is generally a people-centered person—an intuitive, emotional creature—and she longs to share those deep inner thoughts and feelings with her husband. In other words, she wants him to be her best friend.

**Bill:** Is this difficult for a husband? Most definitely. Is it worth it? You bet. It is not that a woman simply wants to talk about herself, although that is important at times. She wants to know her man's deep feelings, his dreams, his hurts, his doubts, his secrets. That establishes a very intimate oneness, and women need that, just as men need to be praised and respected.

### #4. By Noticing Me More—Not Just When He Wants Sex

**Anabel:** This is the only reference to sex in the top twenty. That is not to imply that a good sex life is unimportant to the female. But if the only time a husband notices you is when he wants sex, then you are lowered to being a piece of equipment around the house to be used when needed. That's a pretty good definition of a mistress or a prostitute, isn't it? I'm a wife, not a mistress. I need my husband to elevate me to that position. That means including me all day long in his life as his *partner*, and ultimately including me in the sex act as his *partner*, not as a sex *object*.

**Partner:** "Someone you talk things over with; someone who engages in an activity with another; joint interests" (Webster). Husbands and wives can build together on the foundation of that definition.

### #5. By Saying "Thank You" for the Things I Do

**Anabel:** Expressing thanks has healed many a wound, encouraged many a tired soul, impressed many onlookers (including the kids), and is certainly well-pleasing to God. Let's hear one woman's viewpoint.

*I resent my husband deeply, Anabel. I resent his being gone all of the time; and if he is home, I resent him curling up with his paper on the sofa while I continue with the dishes and kids and clothes and baths, and on and on.*

*I resent it that he can make it to a meeting or to work, but never to anything I would like to do. I resent his haphazard "jumping on the kids" approach to discipline. I resent having to get out of my chair to switch his TV station for him, especially when I've finally just gotten settled and he's closer to the TV anyway!*

*And I resent my kids. I love them—OH! I do love them, but frequently I can't stand them. I guess it's that I resent being a servant to everybody when no one seems to appreciate what I do all that much.*

*And Anabel, if I confront my husband with the way I feel, somehow it always winds up being my fault, and I wind up crying, and Anabel, I am so tired of crying.*

**Bill:** Gratitude goes both ways. Let's listen to a male viewpoint:

*You know, Bill, if the husband gets up every morning and goes to this eight-hour-daily and comes home to nothing but flak—someone yelling at you because you didn't do something they wanted you to do, or because you did something wrong that you tried to do; if all the kids ever do is take and take and take but never say thanks—then one day as you're heading for your eight-hour-daily, YOU'RE GOING TO COME TO A FORK IN THE ROAD!*

*One fork leads to people who see you as a*

*money-machine, who ride you and criticize you and show no gratitude at all for what you do. The other fork leads to freedom. And you know, Bill, you're pretty tempted to take the road that leads to freedom.*

**Anabel:** Being grateful and expressing your gratitude to people—most of all your spouse—works wonders. A husband's gratitude for his wife...
- Makes her feel needed.
- Encourages her to keep going.
- Enhances her sense of self-worth.
- Let others (including the kids) see that you are considerate of her, and she loves that.
- Trains your children to express thanks and to appreciate her contributions to the family.

For all that, she will deeply appreciate you.

**Bill:** Those same things apply to the husband and are just as important to them as they are to wives. Gratitude was, in large part, what was missing in the life of the man who had come to the fork in the road.

### #6. By Being Interested in My Life...at Least Acting Like You're Interested

**Bill:** This brings us back to communication again. Have you talked to people whose eyes wander while you're sharing your ideas with them? It makes you feel like they just aren't that interested. We men have to keep in mind that one of the most effective ways to communicate interest is eye contact.

Another effective tool for showing interest is follow-up. Asking questions on some subject the other party has been discussing demonstrates that you are indeed interested in what he or she has been saying. Try these on your wife:

- "How did your afternoon go at work?"
- "How did your meeting turn out today?"
- "Hey, your hair looks nice. Do you like it?"
- "What did the doctor say about the pain in your back?"
- "Find anything that interested you in your shopping today? Well, try it on, and let me see how it looks." (The shock of this one just might be too much for her to handle!)

Keep this in mind—it makes no difference whether you actually *feel* interested or not. Jesus is interested, and He will express that interest through you if you'll take the first step: acting interested by faith. And do you know what? As you practice this, you'll eventually become interested. It will cease to be an effort and become a habit...a lifestyle. That's called growing in Christ.

### #7. By Showing Affection When Other People Are Around

**Anabel:** What do you do with something that is very precious to you?

- You look at it.
- You touch it.
- You polish it up.
- You check up on it regularly just to be sure all is well with it.
- You like to have it close to you and know exactly where it is.

That's what showing affection to your wife is like. It's

part of that TLC we talked about before. Showing affection to your wife gives her a sense of being protected, being secure, and being precious to you. It makes her feel proud, as if to say, "See? My husband loves me!"

**Bill:** One night we drove up to a restaurant just as another couple arrived. I don't know how old they were, but they were pretty close to being feeble. He came around to her side of the car—ever so slowly—and opened the door for her. She put her arm through his, and they walked leisurely into the restaurant. And, wonder of wonders, they sat down on the same side of the booth, real close. Their behavior communicated tenderness, attentiveness, and closeness. Women never outgrow these needs.

While mowing my lawn a couple of summers ago, I noticed an elderly man walking down our side street; his wife struggled along a half block behind. I left my mower and fell in beside him saying, "Hi! Would you hear a word from a counselor?" "Okay!" he shouted in the manner of old men. I laid my hand on his shoulder. "You know, if you'd slow down and walk with your wife, you'd send her this message: 'I'm so proud that you're my wife. We've had some good years together. Thank you for all the happiness you've brought me. I love you.'" We took a few steps in silence. Then he turned his head and shouted, "She can't keep up!" "I know it. That's why you need to slow down." I smiled at him and went back to my mower. It really makes my day now when I occasionally see them out walking. They actually hold hands!

**Anabel:** I love those stories—but let's move on to...

### #8. By Sharing His Goals and Values with Me; Talking His Business Over with Me
**Anabel:** Young mothers may be the ones who feel this

need most, especially after they've been carrying on not-so-stimulating conversations all day long with toddlers. A young career woman may need it because she wants to unload and she needs some empathy from her mate. An older woman may need it because her nest is empty, and she longs to be a part of her husband's life. All women love it because it gives us a sense that our husbands recognize our intelligence and want us to be a part of their world. A lack of communication about goals and work cuts the wife out of a huge portion of her husband's life.

**Bill:** Discussing important decisions that affect the family welfare should be included here. If a husband has a chance at a job promotion, but it means moving to Arizona—he should talk to his wife about it as soon as possible. If he has an opportunity to become involved in a very lucrative business endeavor, but it seems just a little shady—the two of them need to talk about it before he involves his wife in something that goes against her moral values.

Husbands and wives are one. When a man leaves his wife out of his business dealings, he is not honoring their oneness.

**#9. By Remembering Me with Little Gifts or Just Planning an Evening Out Every So Often**

Two men from our church surprised their wives by buying weekend getaway packages (airfare and hotel at $150.00 per couple). They got sitters for the children, and enlisted the help of a lady friend who coached them on what clothing and makeup to pack and stow away in the trunk of the car.

Finally, the big day arrived. They told their wives they were taking them to dinner at a restaurant on the far side of the Dallas-Ft. Worth Airport. As they passed the terminal building, the driver had to turn in to "make an important phone call." They arrived at curbside check-in just in time to make the 6 p.m. flight to Houston.

Can you picture the women's eyes as they walked arm-in-arm with their husbands to board the plane?

**Anabel:** Any wife would love that! And even though hotel weekends may be out of your price range, that's all right. It isn't that we need the expensive weekend. It's the thought, the effort, and the actual carrying out of the plan that touches us. I know couples who have been married for years, and they still hold tenaciously to a date every week.

### #10. By Taking Me Out Without the Kids More—Maybe Just for a Ride

**Anabel:** Women who mention this really emphasize "without the kids." When a woman goes out with her husband and takes the kids along, the stress factor increases at an exponential rate. It intensifies the pressures that she's been subjected to all day long. She takes her "office work" with her, but can't take the "office equipment" necessary to do her job, and instead of a much-needed diversion, it can actually be an exhausting experience, plus coming home to her same nightly responsibilities.

### #11. By Including Me in the Things He Does

**Anabel:** We were talking about this with a group one time, and a woman remarked, "I don't need to worry about that, Anabel. My husband takes me deer hunting every season…to cook for him and his hunting buddies." That's not what we mean! Men may take their wives along for all the wrong reasons—to be a servant, a sex partner, or an audience.

A wife longs to be taken as a companion.

Even if she is unable to physically accompany him, her husband can make her feel so very special by saying things like: "Traveling is no fun without you. When I see interesting things I'm thinking, 'If only you were here to share this with me.' When I eat out at some fancy place, I just think how much nicer it would be to have you there with me." These comments help a wife feel included even when she can't actually be there every time.

### #12. By Trying to Understand Me
**Bill:** Here's that "Let's plant a big garden" concept again—intuition verses logic. Do you know what those words mean?

- Logic: way of reasoning; what is expected by the working of cause and effect.
- Intuition: the immediate knowing of something without the conscious use of reasoning.

**Anabel:** When I tell Bill that I "feel" a certain way about something, my attempts at explaining *why* are sometimes lacking. I don't generally do that very well. Women love for men to at least try to "understand them," and it sometimes takes a lot of concentrated effort.

### #13. By Getting Involved with Things I Enjoy Doing
**Anabel:** As little girls we used to play dress-up, and we never could get the boys to play with us. Most women still enjoy playing dress-up, and we still have trouble getting our "boy" to play. That means going somewhere in all of my finery—with him in his. Maybe even the ballet!

**Bill:** Yes, I confess. I now dress up and go to the ballet. But, at least I had the self-respect to wait until John Wayne died!

Your wife will be unique. Maybe she loves to square dance, or go for bike rides on the bike trail, or play volleyball, or walk hand in hand on the beach, or play games with just you and another couple.

Wives are often admonished to "get involved," to watch ball games with their men, to go water-skiing with them, look at their guns and be impressed with their tales of conquest. Okay, it's our turn now, guys. It spices up the marriage for both of us when I get involved with some of the things my wife likes to do. However, having a spiced-up marriage cannot be my motivation. The goal of Christ's Life is never self, but others. I am to let Him love my wife through me, meeting these very special needs that only I can satisfy.

Let me interject an admonition here. As Anabel and I discuss the needs of the wife, Sgt. Sin may be "saying" to the woman reader, "Oh Lord, pour it on him! I'm so glad he's hearing this." Sin will work the same number on the husband: "Lord, You sure have her where You want her now. Sock it to her!"

This book is not written for your spouse to read so that you can get your needs met. It's for you to read so that you, in turn, can offer yourself to Christ as a servant to meet your spouse's needs. Christ lives to serve, not survive. Serving your spouse will make you a winner in His eyes.

### #14. By Just Holding Me in His Arms and Talking to Me

**Anabel:** This letter really says it all:

*When my husband came home from work yesterday, the house was a wreck and the kids were driving me wild. When I told him I just couldn't handle it, do you know what he did? He took me out into the laundry room, put his hands on my shoulders, looked down into my face and said very quietly, "Now, just calm down." Then he put his arms around me, pulled me against him and just held me for five whole minutes without saying a word. I can't explain to you how good it felt to be in his arms like that. I began to slowly relax and escape from my stressed-out world.*

*Then he said, "Now let's tackle this and see if we can get those little 'buzz saws' fed and into bed early tonight. Then we'll get a sitter and you and I will go to that quiet little pizza place and be together, just you and me."*

Protection. Attention. Being loved. Closeness without passion. Security. Safety from the "cold north winds" that blow about the house. Encirclement in arms that are strong. This is what women are asking for, longing for, praying for. Are their men listening?

### #15. By Being Tender—Using Kind, Tender Words
**Bill:** Many men develop the macho mind-set during childhood and never stop to realize how destructive it can be. A physically big man may consider it beneath himself to be tender; a physically small man may be too threatened to be tender. A plain vanilla man may have been "trained like a bird dog" that to be tender is to be a sissy. "Don't ever cry. Don't ever let your feelings show. Don't stoop to being soft."

**Anabel:** Men of all personalities need to understand that women thrive on tenderness. Tenderness not only causes us to respect their masculinity all the more, but to admire their sensitivity as well.

### #16. By Helping in the Discipline of the Children
**Anabel:** Being with children all day is part of a woman's job description. And she programs an awful lot of things into them during her nine hours a day, in contrast to the three or four hours they spend with their

father in the evenings. Wives want their husbands to realize that and to respect it.

**Bill:** It's important for fathers to understand that they shouldn't march in with an all new set of rules after work every day. If you worked under one boss from 7:30 a.m. until 6:30 p.m., and then had another person come in and set up entirely different standards and procedures, you'd be confused and frustrated. That's how your wife and kids feel if you come home each evening with a different way of doing things. The two of you must be united before the kids. Settle differences later.

**Anabel:** Parents need to work together and be consistent in whatever they do with the children. Wives, don't cut your husband out of the children's lives through the day. And don't use him as the "big, bad bear" who is going to appear around dark and "then you kids will be sorry!"

Allow the children to see that you respect your husband, that you are under his authority just as they are under yours, and that you don't wear the pants in the family. Your sons and daughters need to see that you and your husband agree about the important issues in life, and especially those where they are concerned.

A wife feels secure when the children understand that if they sass her, they answer to her husband. How I admired the man who said to his rebellious teenage son, "You're not going to treat my wife that way." A wife really knows whose side her husband is on if he says something like that.

On the other hand, communication about the children sometimes sounds more like this:

Wife: "Something is bothering Junior."

Husband: "How do you know that?"

Wife: "He's been throwing his toys, and trying to kick Cissy. I can just tell that he's upset about something."

Husband: "Oh, you're always getting these ideas. Just forget it."

Wife: "But, dear, he needs our help."

Husband: "He'll grow out of it."

Wise parents accomplish oneness in the area of discipline through that magic word "communication." They talk things through after the kids are in bed. Perhaps they disagree at times, but they are determined to present that united front both morning and night. A wife really does need that. For that matter, so does her husband.

### #17. By Saying Little Words of Caring, Compliments, and Appreciation

**Anabel:** By noticing and saying the little things, husbands are powerfully communicating the big things. Bill often tells me that he loves me (caring), that he thinks I'm really great, that he appreciates me for who I am (compliments), and that he is well aware of all I do (appreciation). All of these build my sense of self-worth and make me feel loved.

As we're both getting ready for work, he might say, "Wow, that suit really does you right." He might notice a clean house. Or that dinner was particularly tasty. Or that I've completed a project he asked me to do. It's simple really, husbands just need to open their eyes and speak up.

**Bill:** Even though, as Christians, we ought to have our sense of self-worth focused on who we are in Christ Jesus, it surely makes life a lot nicer if our spouses meet our earthly needs for praise with encouraging and appreciative words.

### #18. By Accepting Me Just As I Am

**Anabel:** This request covers my physical appearance, my performance, my achievements, my character, my mannerisms…all of the things that make me who I am. I met a woman for lunch one day. We both ordered French onion soup, but when she began telling me about what was happening in her marriage, neither of us touched our soup.

She sadly related to me that her husband had a habit of picking out some woman and making several positive comments about her, such as, "I really like the way she wears her hair. Why don't you fix yours that way, Nancy?" Nancy would find out where the woman had her hair done, go to the shop, and say, "Fix it like hers."

The husband would never notice.

He did the same thing with clothes, even shoes. He never overtly said to her, "You don't measure up to the women I admire," but it was communicated to her very painfully by inference.

**Bill:** Husbands must earn the right to point out their wives' mistakes and faults by demonstrating a lifestyle of consistent encouragement. We earn that right by saying caring words, by giving compliments, and by expressing appreciation. When we do this faithfully, our wives will be better able to receive our occasional constructive suggestions.

### #19. By Spending More Time with the Family

**Bill:** Does it sound like we're contradicting ourselves when we say on the one hand, "Take your wife out without the kids more often," and on the other, "Spend more time with the family"? We're not. Your wife definitely needs time away from the children. But it thrills her when you plan family outings, when you agree to take little Clair for her dancing lessons, when you manage to be there for Junior's soccer game, when you take your son fishing, or when you shoot baskets with your daughter.

I've counseled enough to know what happens to a family with an absentee father. Listen, talk about waking up someday with a regret the size of Dallas! I don't want that, and I know that you don't want that either. You love your children just as I do. Remember the old saying, "An ounce of prevention is worth a pound of cure"? What a tragedy it would be to have to look back one day and say, "If only...."

## #20. By Making Me Feel Like a Woman

**Anabel:** When Adam said, "This is now bone of my bones, and flesh of my flesh; She shall be called woman..." (Genesis 2:23), I imagine that Eve *felt* like something very special. She felt feminine, not like just another animal in the garden menagerie. And I imagine that she sometimes caught Adam looking at her during the course of the day, and she re-experienced that same feeling.

I suppose "feeling desirable" would describe what women are requesting. Desirable means, "worth having; pleasing." I'm quite capable of opening a car door, but when Bill opens it for me, or when he helps me with my chair, I can't help but feel that I'm "special" to him.

A male still likes to feel masculine even when he is eighty years old. We women are no different. My need to feel feminine does not somehow disappear once I'm married, or when the kids are grown and gone, or when I'm eighty years old. No, I'll need to feel like a woman until the day I die.

I'm always reminded of the story of my auntie. She was an eighty-six-year-old widow and we were shopping for a bra. Quite frankly, I had never seen an 86 year old earthsuit and hers was one big wrinkle. I had decided that we needed a firm, heavy bra to give support, so I started picking out samples and taking them to the dressing room for her to try. She kept rejecting them and I finally said, "What kind do you want, Blanchie?" Her answer illustrates the point I've been trying to make, "Oh, I want something *feminine*, Honey...."

## Important Words for Special Women

An angry young woman approached me one night after we had been discussing the needs of women in a seminar. Essentially, this is what she said, "My husband is my husband in name only, Anabel. I've been getting along as well as could be expected, but you have torn open my heart and uncovered all of these hidden desires. I never knew what was causing my unhappiness and the turbulence in my soul. Now you have made me aware of these needs, and my emotions are screaming at me for tenderness and companionship and all of the things that I will never have! I would have been better off if I had never known!"

On another occasion, I was reading the *Family Weekly* periodical, and came across an interview with the renowned author, Taylor Caldwell. When asked if the nine-hour TV production of her book, *Captains and Kings*, would bring her solid satisfaction, she replied: "There is no solid satisfaction in any career for a woman like myself. There is no home, no true freedom, no hope, no joy, no expectation for tomorrow, no contentment. I would rather cook a meal for the man I love and bring him his slippers and feel myself in the protection of his arms than have all the citations and awards and honors I have received worldwide, including the Ribbon of Legion of Honor, and my properties and my bank accounts. They mean nothing to me, and I am only one among the millions of sad women like myself."

Many of you women who are reading this live as these

women live: you are an unhappy single woman, you are a widow, you are a single-again woman, you are a woman whose husband is not truly loving her at all. What are you to do? Are you to suffer through life without having your need for tenderness met? Without a companion? Without being loved? Cherished? Respected? Can these deep needs be met only by a physical husband, an earthly mate?

Oh, my dear ones, is Christ limited and unable to satisfy this need for you?

> *Looking upon them, Jesus said, "With men it is impossible, but not with God; for all things are possible with God"* (Mark 10:27).

He is able. You are His beloved bride and He longs to meet your every need. I can walk with the poise and confidence of a woman who knows she is loved and cherished. I can accept all the exquisite gifts that my Husband so lovingly sends to me (be they wild flowers, clouds, trees, or birds...). I can walk with Him and I can talk with Him and I can hear Him say, "You are mine and I love you deeply." How I cherish the thought of every person, man or woman, who walks alone, unloved in the world, grasping and clinging tenaciously to the indescribable, unsurpassed, constant, and tender love of the Bridegroom, Jesus Christ.[1]

---

[1]For further teaching on this beautiful truth, please read Chapter 13 of *The Confident Woman*, by Anabel Gillham (Harvest House Publishers, Eugene, Oregon, 1993).

# How Wives Spell Love

*Once I began to allow Christ to use me to express verbal love to Anabel, He began to reveal new and creative ways to say, "I love you."*

# Chapter Twelve

Dear Anabel,

I can only begin this letter by saying that if the pain that we are all now suffering were physical, I'm sure the wound would be fatal. It never ceases to amaze me how much emotional trauma one can withstand.

Our last counselor told Mike that as long as he had someone to lean on, he would. Hopefully, on his own he will find the self-motivation he needs. I love my husband very much and am as concerned for his well-being as I am for my own and the children's, but I'm just so weary. My self-survival alarm is buzzing and manifesting itself in weight loss, amnesia, and sleeplessness.

I feel guilty and somewhat selfish to be the one to say, "I quit," but I am scared and don't really know what else to do. If only this could be what Mike needs. I know the conflict between our needs and the fact that neither of us is able to satisfy those needs is destroying both of us, regardless of how much we still love each other. It is as though we are groping and drowning in our pain, fear, and frustration, reaching out to each other for help, but our arms just aren't long enough to bridge the gap. And if you tread water long enough, the fear of sinking eventually changes to a blessed relief and you no longer fear it, but welcome it.

I have shortchanged Mike in many ways, too. It's a vicious circle. Mike doesn't satisfy my needs as a husband or father on a daily "let's function together and get it done" basis. I don't like it when I carry all the responsibilities, so I build resentment toward him. This reduces my ability to give and show him the affection and praise he so desperately needs. Therefore he escapes and seeks it elsewhere, leaving me back where we started, doing it alone. It's an 'I will if you will' situation, but it has reached the point where neither of us can, let alone will.

At first I had such horrible doubts: What about the kids, what about money, will Mike be all right, can he get up with an alarm, can he find his own socks, and for heaven's sake, can I withstand the pain when the kids ask why Daddy lives somewhere else?

Through the bedroom window I can see the plum tree full of green leaves. A month ago it was just a stump with dry, bare branches, but spring

*came just like it always does. I'm sure that spring
will come again for us and that after this winter is
over we can be fruitful again. We just need some
time to trim and prune. We already have two blos-
soms that need us both, but not as we are now. I'll
close with this thought: "Please Lord, teach us to
laugh again. But God, don't ever let us forget that
we cried."*

**Anabel:** It's pretty obvious that Mike doesn't know
how his wife spells love. Even if he does know, he has no
idea where to get the power to meet her needs. There must
be millions of marriages with problems similar to this one.

As Christians, we have some very specific instructions
from God about marriage. His Word says...

> *Husbands, love your wives, just as Christ also loved
> the church and gave Himself up for her; that He
> might sanctify her, having cleansed her by the wash-
> ing of water with the word, that He might present
> himself to the church in all her glory, having no spot
> or wrinkle or any such thing; but that she should be
> holy and blameless* (Ephesians 5:25-27).

**Bill:** That's the way I'm commanded to love Anabel.
This means far more than having warm, fuzzy feelings
toward her, doesn't it? Look at the pronouns in the passage
above. The church is referred to as "her." We husbands are
to take our cues for loving our wives from Jesus' relationship to His wife.

**Anabel:** Just what was it Jesus gave His wife as an
expression of His love? He gave "Himself." That's what
husbands are to give to wives. Oh, they can go along with
all of the suggestions we've already given, and they can
master the other ones we're going to give. But none of it

will be satisfying nor fulfilling to their women if they do not first give themselves. Otherwise, those other truths will become laws that men do out of obligation. And wives will sense that their hubsands are either trying to appease or manipulate.

**Bill:** But wives, you must be very sensitive. I've talked with women whose husbands have communicated to them, "I want to please you. I want to try to meet your needs. Please believe me." That's "giving himself." What should the wife do now? She should encourage him and help him, understanding that his emotions probably won't come along right at the first, but *at least he is trying*.

That wife must be very aware that Satan will be fighting to keep her marriage from healing and just might give her such thoughts as, "He doesn't really mean it. He's faking it. I'd rather him not do it than to so obviously be forcing himself. I don't want love that way."

Now wait a minute. He has told you the desire of his heart. Right? Evaluate your own performance. Do you have an "Oh! What fun this is!" mentality about some of the things you do for him? Are your emotions on an eight or ten with joy when you're doing some of the mundane things for him that you know please him? No.

Your hubby is trying. Help him out.

**Anabel:** I remember one woman who sat in my office with diamonds in her ears, on her fingers, and around her neck. Her beautiful mink coat was thrown over the back of the chair. Her face was buried in her arms and her body was shaking with sobs. Finally, she raised her head, lifted her chin defiantly, looked disdainfully at all her adornments and said, "Look at me, Anabel. I'm loved."

I have often said that I would rather be under the direction of Ephesians 5:22 than under that of Ephesians 5:25. Men very obviously have the more difficult responsibility.

God's word to the wife is "Submit."

God's word to the husband is "DIE."

**Bill:** Notice the phrase, "gave Himself up." How many rights does a man have who gives himself up for someone? None.

It is entirely possible for me to admire Anabel, and feel deep romantic attachment to her, and yet be ignorant of just how to agape her as Christ agapes His wife. But as I "give myself up" to Him, He can give Himself up through me, and I can love her His way. Now I can't give up my rights in my own strength, but Christ can do it through me.

### Learning to Love from Jesus

**Anabel:** Because this is such a powerful concept, Bill and I have searched the Scriptures in order to understand it more thoroughly. We have discovered six ways that we believe Christ loves His wife, the Church. Let's apply these spiritual concepts to our practical, daily living. Over the course of the next chapters, you'll find all six of these principles spelled out. They describe the deep commitment Jesus has to His Bride. And Bill and I will try to make some suggestions as to how husbands can "life them out." Here's the first...

## 1. JESUS LONGS FOR HER TO KNOW JUST HOW MUCH HE LOVES HER

### A Husband With a Stuck Feeler

**Bill:** How can I emulate Christ's love to let my wife know just how much I love her? Well, how about simply telling her, "I love you"? That may sound easy, but I've counseled men who couldn't say the "L" word to their wives.

I remember one man who had told his wife ten years before that if he ever stopped loving her he'd let her know.

That's as tender and loving a message as he could muster up in order to express love to his wife.

**Anabel:** I talked to his wife. Her perception was so much different. She looked at me with tears in her eyes and said, "Anabel, my husband hasn't told me that he loves me in ten years!"

**Bill:** Why would saying "I love you" be so hard for him to do? He would probably explain that it just runs in his family, that none of his relatives ever said "I love you" to each other, or to their wives or to their children, and that he's just like his father and his brothers. He views it as genetic!

Well, it's not genetic—his feeler is stuck.

This man probably considers himself unlovely and unworthy of either giving or receiving love. Or perhaps he received the verbal and emotional message as a child that "real" males never say the "L" word, and therefore he is unable to express love to others. He can't give what he doesn't have. His emotions have stayed lined up on that perception for so long that they've eventually become stuck. On a one-to-ten scale he now *feels* inhibited about verbalizing love at level eight even on his best days! If he ever tried to say, "I love you," he'd *feel* like a big phony. He just can't do it. But Christ through him is able. By letting Christ use him this way, he would be far from being a phony…he'd be obedient.

## "I Don't Want to Be a Hypocrite"

I recall another man, a dedicated Christian, who had not told his wife he loved her in over twenty years. Much like the other man, he had been rejected in childhood. At about age eleven he was walking home from school with a worldly woman of twelve who suggested it might be fun for them to kiss each other. He agreed, and gave her a peck on the cheek.

She said, "No! *This* is the way you kiss!" She proceeded to kiss him square on the mouth till the bells went off. He'd never felt anything so zingy in all his born days! As years went by, he searched the whole world over to find a female who could consistently make the "bells of St. Mary's" go off when he kissed her. He never did.

He eventually got married, but deep down, he *felt* like he had missed the "right" woman. Consequently, he didn't *feel* as though he really loved his wife, so he could never tell her that he did. That would make him *feel* like a phony, and he couldn't handle that *feeling*. Consequently, his wife lived with him for over twenty years but never heard those words she longed with all her heart to hear.

God didn't command me to express my love to Anabel when I "feel" like it. He simply said that I was to do it.

"But Bill, if I were to tell my wife that I love her when in fact I don't *feel* love for her, that would make me a hypocrite, wouldn't it?" Well, let's examine the definition of the word hypocrite and find out. Hypocrite actually means *Pretending to be what one is not* (Webster). However, the Deceiver has his own definition: *Acting contrary to how you feel.* That's a lie!

As one would suspect, the world subscribes to the Deceiver's definition. And alas, most Christians, even many Christian counselors, apparently do as well. They focus their emphasis on what your feeler "says." Counselors tell us to "get in touch with our feelings" as though emotions were our primary barometer of truth. We are told that expressing our true feelings is being honest, and that if we don't have the feelings we once had for our spouse, it is dishonest to stay in the marriage. Our modern world wants us to be controlled by our fickle feelers...*a part of us that can't even think!*

But remember—Christ is your Life (see Colossians

3:4a). If you claim, by faith, that Christ is expressing His Life through you, and then say to your wife, "I love you, Susie," would you be pretending to be what you are not? Or would you be acting as if something is true which really *is* true? You'd be "walking in the light" instead of being controlled by your emotions. You'd be letting Jesus verbalize love to your wife through you. And your feeler would ultimately begin to respond.

## Appropriating Christ as Life

By way of illustration, you can know all there is to know about how to operate your computer, and you can type on your keyboard to your heart's content. However, if you never turn the computer on, your typing will be powerless. There's a simple exercise that can help you appropriate Christ as Life, enabling you to overcome.

**Step One:** *Claim your power*—the "Spirit of Christ" as Life (the Holy Spirit) by faith. You don't need more faith. You use the same faith you used to get saved. Then you claimed Him as Savior and Lord; now you're claiming Him as Life. This "turns the switch on."

You pray, "Jesus I surrender all that I am to You so that You, in turn, can express Your Life through me. I mean this with every fiber of my being. I give up—no strings, no deals, no hidden agenda on my part. You take over and do Your will through me."

**Step Two:** Get up off your knees believing that the "Spirit of Christ" is now expressing His Life through you. And begin to *act like it's true.* This is where the power lies in living the Christian life. If you wait until you "feel" Him start living through you, you'll never get off dead center. It's done by faith and obedience, not by *feeling.*

## "I Love You, Susie!"

I have found that to jump right in and say, "I love you,

Susie," is a tough assignment for a man whose feeler is stuck, but we can make it easier.

If you're one of those guys, stretch your emotions slowly. First, set your watch alarm for 2:00 a.m. Lie there in the dark staring at the ceiling, and say, "Okay, Lord, here goes. You're going to do this through me. Ready?" And you whisper, "I love you, Susie." Susie is still sawing logs, but that's okay. You've started the ball rolling, and Christ did it for you, through you! You're on a roll!

Next time, trust Christ to write it to her through you. Then trust Him to tell her through you over the phone. Then holler it from the car as you drive away. You'll finally get to where you can actually look her in the eyes and say those words: "I love you, Susie."

Aw, come on, brother, do it! Stand against the devil and be God's man. The Deceiver is keeping you from loving your wife through your stuck feeler, and you don't want to let him keep making a monkey of you. Fight like the new man you are in Christ! Keep working at tenderness and believe, by faith, that Christ is tearing down those strongholds which you have developed and strengthened over the years by playing "lord of the ring."

Christ will do it, man. It may not happen in a big flash of light, and that's all right. No man totally overcomes the flesh on this planet. But as you practice this process and time progresses, you'll get more and more freedom from those lifelong hang-ups. You'll love the results and so will your wife.

But what if you continue to let Sgt. Sin control you through your feelings? What if you persist in being clammed up? Now you are "pretending to be what you are *not." That makes you a phony* by God's definition. A hypocrite. You are acting differently from who God says you are in Christ, and every time your image stares back at you from your mirror you'll have to confess, "I'm a phony."

You don't want to live like that! Come on. Give up and sell out to Christ as Life. That's why God led you to this book. You're looking for an answer to help your marriage, and now you've found it. *Christ living through you is your answer.*

## "I Don't Want to Be Critical, But..."

**Anabel:** Women say to me, "Anabel, I don't want to be critical of my husband. He's a good man and has always provided well for our family. But I so yearn for gentleness, for tenderness, for him to touch me and tell me that he loves me.

"You will probably laugh at me or think I am terrible, but watching my teenage daughter get ready for a date has created such discontent in my relationship with my husband. I actually envy her at times. I'm not too old to dress up and go out on the town, and oh, how I would love it!"

**Bill:** You know, sometimes we males don't hear very well. My wife might be telling me that she wants to "put on the dog" and go do the town at level ten. But I hear her telling me at level two. I have found it very helpful for Anabel to put a number on her requests. For instance, when she says, "Bill, I'd like for you to get the battery in my car fixed and that's a nine," it communicates to me that I should jump on it and get it done.

Once I began to allow Christ to use me to express verbal love to Anabel, He began to reveal new and creative ways to say, "I love you." I don't mean in French, but in actions! Actions really do speak louder than words.

I recall a time when it was our son Will's birthday. We make a big deal of birthdays in our family by loading the birthday person down with gifts. We also limit gift giving at Christmas in order to load Jesus down on His birthday.

At any rate, Will had expressed a desire for a certain gift. Anabel wanted to get it, but I didn't think we should. Later, I realized she was right, so I went down and purchased it without telling her. On birthday morning, I slipped the secret package into the pile and then sat back to watch both Will's and Anabel's reactions. As he picked it up, her brow furrowed in curiosity because she didn't recognize the package.

Anabel was shocked when Will opened the gift. She quickly looked at me, smiled, and her eyes began to brim up a little. It was then that the Holy Spirit let me know that I had just said to her, "I love you, Anabel." Until it happened, I hadn't known that this was a way to tell my wife that I loved her.

There must be dozens of ways to "say" to our wives, "I love you." But unless I hold a funeral for my old ways and allow Christ to begin to live His Life through me, I may never discover them.

Another key principle we learned from studying about Christ's love for His Bride is that…

## 2. SHE IS HIS CONSUMING DESIRE

**Anabel:** Let's place this second way Christ loves His Bride on an attainable level. If women had the opportunity, they would say, "Find ways to let me know that I am often on your mind."

### "You're Always on My Mind"

Bill has done such a beautiful job of this over the years. He has trained the boys to do the same, which means I am very blessed. It all began when our sons were little, and they'd go out hiking or fishing to the woods with their dad. Invariably, one of them would bring me a rock from their trip. I don't mean a polished rock; I mean a creek pebble. Now, just what did that little pebble communicate to me? "Here's something for you, Mom, to let you know that I was thinking about you while we were gone."

I remember one of the most delightful things Bill ever did to show me he was thinking of me. He came home one day from a trip and said, "I brought you something." That was almost to be expected because he is so good that way, but the "something" was generally in a corner of his suitcase wrapped securely in his dirty clothes. But this time it was a big box—probably two cubic feet. I couldn't imagine! You know what it was? A huge pumpkin! I loved it!

Now some woman may be thinking, "So what was he saying...make some pumpkin pies?" Wrong. My men rarely bring me remembrances from the jewelry store or the department store. You see, they have *listened* to me over the years...they know me...and they know what I like. Tucked in my Bible are some very delicate little feathers and a sprig of greenery from a redwood tree in Yosemite. I have some black bean pods on the buffet and some stuffed animals that have come to live with us. All of these things say, "You were on my mind."

**Bill:** Calling your wife from work during the day also lets her know you're thinking of her. The call says "I love you" or "I am praying for you" or "I know you're struggling a little right now and I want you to know I care." Just talking to her...calls that say "Have you picked up my cleaning yet," or "How much money is in the household account?" don't count, guys.

I might also call and say, "Hey, how about meeting for lunch at Whataburger?"

If Anabel and I are in a motel doing a seminar, on my morning run I could pick a little wildflower and put it in a glass by the lavatory. When Anabel turns on the light that little wildflower will greet her. She likes things like that.

**Anabel:** Those kinds of things prove to me that Bill knows how I spell love. He is thinking about me when we're apart. I occupy a very important place in his life. Little gifts like the wildflower are evidence to me that he knows me...that he really listens to me. If I were to put a number on how much things like that mean to me it would be a ten. All of these things we are discussing are tens to me.

This is how my husband is to love me. In fact, this is the way all husbands are to love their wives. God created women with these special needs, and He desires that every husband meet those needs by offering himself up to Christ as a "living sacrifice."

# HAVE YOU NOTICED YOUR WIFE LATELY?

*How long has it been since you have said to your wife, "You look so pretty tonight, Sweetheart"?*

# $\sim$ Chapter Thirteen $\sim$

**A**nabel: How does Christ love His bride? We've seen that He longs to communicate his love to her. And yes, He thinks about her constantly. And...

## 3. EVERY WORD, EVERY ACTION BRINGS HONOR AND EXPRESSES HIS DEVOTION TO HER

It would seem that we are looking at the impossible. How can a husband devote his every action and word to his wife? Putting it on a practical level makes it a far more obtainable goal: "Husband, *listen* to your wife and *share* your life with her."

*Dear Anabel,*

*I guess I just need someone to help me understand what's going on. Let me try to explain. It's my job to take care of the washing at home, and I'm not complaining about that. But my washing machine broke. I told my husband about it and he suggested that I go to the neighborhood laundry for a while because he didn't "have the time to look into it just now." A couple of weeks later, I mentioned it to him again and he, rather gruffly, agreed to check it out. He's really handy with things like that. It needed a new part, so he called and ordered one from Sears. It arrived a week later, but it was the wrong part. He finally got around to ordering the replacement. It came about a week ago and is still in the box in the garage.*

*Now here is my dilemma.*

*My husband came home from work and told me how his secretary's computer had gone on the blink at 10:00 that morning and how he had called the office machines' repair shop and told them to get over there on the double—"We have some important mail to get out." They didn't come, so he called back and told them that if they weren't coming to repair it they should bring him a replacement. "We can't get our work done around here without it."*

*He is not in love with his secretary. She's a super secretary, he tells me that regularly, but that is not the issue. What bothers me is that her work is so important and mine is not. When the "tools" I need to get my work done break, he doesn't set any records repairing them.*

*The only way I can put all this together is that*

*what I do must not be very important to my husband. He doesn't seem to notice, and he doesn't listen when I talk to him about it or fix "my tools" when I tell him that they're broken.*

## Give Her Your Full Attention

**Bill:** That husband wasn't paying much attention to his wife's requests, was he? Bless his heart, he probably sees no correlation between fixing the washer and loving his wife. He probably thinks loving her is expressed in the bedroom. How can I show Anabel that I am listening? This is something I have had to work at, and though I haven't arrived yet, it's exciting to me that the Lord has granted me some growth in this area.

First of all, I can make eye contact. I can give Anabel my undivided attention. This means getting away from the ball game on TV or laying my paper down while we talk. Even though I may be really listening as I watch the news, I have learned that when it is important to prove to Anabel that she has my full attention I need to turn the sound off, turn my back to the television set, or walk out of the room with her.

As I trust Christ to live His Life through me, the Holy Spirit will make me sensitive to the times when doing this is necessary. I must refuse to see this as "silly" and realize it is all a part of loving my wife. It's very important that I change my views to conform to those of Christ in me.

## Don't Just Listen, Do Something

Another thing I can do is take some action on whatever concern Anabel discusses with me. For instance, our lawn is sodded with St. Augustine grass and is heavily shaded. I have learned by listening to Anabel that she likes a pretty lawn. One of the ways I say "I love you" is by working on the lawn.

She has mentioned on a couple of occasions that she's concerned because a large area under one of the trees is getting barren looking. She's wondered aloud if we don't need to do something about it.

Anabel overhears me making phone calls to nurseries that handle grass sod, checking on prices, on which strain of grass they recommend, and on how much to water it in order to ensure that it will live. Then she hears me announce that I am going to resod the bare spot under the tree.

The following Saturday I conscript a couple of helpers (sons), hook up the trailer, drive off with my two helpers staring glassy-eyed into the sunrise, return with a load of grass sod, and cover the big bare spot.

What does all this "say" to Anabel?

**Anabel:** You've no idea how many different things that says to me. The main one is, of course, that Bill actually listened to me and heard me. Then, he considered what I said important. Finally, he gave my problem some thought, and now he's going to take action.

There is such a deep emotion that wells up within a woman when she sees her husband walking through the house with his screwdriver in his hand. He's fixing the nest! And that's what his visit to the nursery said to me: "He's fixing the nest." How many women have said to me in different ways, "If only my husband would take some interest in our home." It builds a oneness. It fosters security.

## Understanding Her Love for the Children

**Bill:** At times, when they were young, Anabel would share with me some concern she had about one of the boys. Maybe she didn't get good vibes from a new friend one of them was hanging out with, and she wanted me to talk to him about it.

I'd give it some thought for a couple of days. Then I would come back to her and reopen the conversation, "You know when you mentioned your apprehension over Wade's friend the other day? I've been thinking and praying about it, and I have an idea." Then I'd proceed to share my idea with her. She might or might not have agreed that my idea was a good one, but the episode communicated that I cared about her, and about our boys.

**Anabel:** There is a different bond between a mother and her children than there is between a father and his children. Solomon stripped bare a mother's heart when he suggested cutting her baby in half to settle an argument. God says, "Can a woman forget her nursing child, and have no compassion on the son of her womb? Even these may forget, but I will not forget you" (Isaiah 49:15). He's saying that it is incredulous that a woman would forget her child. There's a special attachment.

When my husband is sensitive to that fusion and is attentive to my thoughts about one of our kids, it meets a deep, deep need in my life. How many times I have said, "Could I talk to you about the boys for just a few minutes?" What I'm saying is, "I sense a problem, and I want you to be involved. I want you to take me seriously."

## Meeting Emotional Needs—At Home

**Bill:** You know, we males can get every one of our basic needs met (with the exception of sex) right out there in the world and still pass as "godly men" in most churches. We can get our need for authority, praise, significance, or achievement satisfied by the world, and most folks will never know how we are depriving our wives of the love God has commanded that we give them.

I can be a physician and have the mothers in town referring to me as "dear old Dr. Bill." That feels great! Or I can run the motor pool at the office and have the sales force bowing to earn my favor, even those who make twice the salary I make. The flesh grooves on that! I can be a cop and hear the important man in the Lincoln calling me "Sir" as I write him up. The flesh loves it!

All of these things can satisfy the masculine needs I have. But if I play the game this way, the flesh, being fickle, requires that each new year (or even each new week) must bring me greater and greater satisfaction from the world. This is one of the major catalysts that produce the mid-life crisis in some men. They're searching for the ultimate masculine flesh trip, and tragically, many believers are searching through psychotherapy for its world-system answer to the problem.

God's answer is that the man must come to the end of himself and his fleshly techniques for getting his needs met.

Now, whereas I, as a male, am able to meet my needs carnally via the world system, Anabel (as a female) cannot typically satisfy her feminine needs through gaining ever-increasing power in the world. God has so designed the wife that her needs are optimally satisfied through her husband, the main man in her life. The typical new woman in Christ isn't tempted by the authority game as we males are. My wife needs me to love her as Christ loves His wife, and if I don't do that, I am sinning against her and against God.

Admittedly, more and more women are into the authority-praise-significance-achievement game, but I have generally found that these women were reared in an environment where pressure for high achievement was either applied by their folks, or they applied it to themselves. It was the key to getting love and self-esteem in their childhood environment, whether spoken or implied, and they are still striving to satisfy their need for self-acceptance through achievement. That's their flesh, not their spirit.

## Living on Emotional Crumbs

**Anabel:** I remember a couple we were talking with in their luxurious home. The husband was venting his wrath, and at the height of his tirade he flung his arm out in the direction of the lavish rooms and said, "Look at everything I have given you! You don't want for a thing! And all I ask from you is sex, and you won't give it to me!

She looked at him with tears running down her cheeks and said, "Is that all you need me for? I would gladly give up all of this just to have you."

That man was getting all of his needs met out in the world system, except his need for physical fulfillment. He couldn't understand why his wife resisted his advances and began to withdraw from him. Begin to take notice in your world…a woman may leave money and social prestige for a man who can offer her nothing but a very small house with a chain link fence. Why? Because he loves her.

**Bill:** I don't mean to be critical of any Christian brother, but there is a unique occupation which affords the male a golden opportunity to feed his need for authority and female praise, and that is the pastorate. How many men, with hearts seeking to please the Lord, put in a seventy-to-ninety hour work week at the church, only to come home at 9:00 p.m. too tired even to toss their faithful wives a few TLC crumbs? These pastors have poured out all their TLC supply on the church.

I believe Jesus is saying to these well-meaning brothers, "You are spending too much time with *My* wife. I instructed you to pour your life into your wife as well as

Mine (see Ephesians 5:25-27), but you're spending so much time with My wife that you have no time for your own."

Many wives of church staffers are starving for the love that God has commanded their husbands to give them, but the husbands are too busy giving it to their work. A man must come to the end of himself on this if he is to go on with God. Let's face it, male flesh finds it stimulating and fulfilling to get its needs for authority and praise satisfied from a smorgasbord of women in the church rather than from only one. Tragically, the flesh being what it is, this scene can evolve into sexual sin in literally "the twinkling of an eye."

## Committing Emotional Adultery

**Anabel:** We call it "emotional adultery" when a husband gives of himself emotionally to other women all day long to the extent that when he gets home, he's too emotionally drained to listen to his wife's problems or be sensitive to her needs.

Let's think this through. Someone is going to have to suffer, either those you counsel, your staff, the secretary who may be sharing her marital problems with you through many tears...or your wife. Who is your God-given responsibility? You are setting your wife up for the mailman who comes by and says, "It's always nice to get to your house, Mrs. Jones. You make my day with your friendliness."

**Bill:** God's Word to the first husband on planet Earth was that his wife was to be his number one responsibility among humans, and that he was even to "leave his father and his mother, and cleave to his wife" in order to accomplish this (Genesis 2:24). He said this before there were even fathers and mothers, and it hasn't changed. I am to seek Jesus first (see Philippians 3:10), but Anabel, not my work nor my ministry, comes second. Everyone else follows Anabel.

## "Other People Are Depending on Me"

I have counseled many folks who were rejected by a dad who naively poured his life into his work and neglected his family. Some were pastors. One woman who came to see me had spent all her formative years seeking her busy-in-the-church dad's attention. She'd even given up high school ball games in order to study and attain the good grades she hoped would please him. And her efforts were well-rewarded—she was named valedictorian!

She practiced diligently for her address at the graduation exercises. "Dad's going to be there. He'll be so proud of me." Remember now, we're talking about an eighteen-year-old young woman who has sacrificed her own pleasure for years to attain this goal.

Well, Dad wasn't there. He missed his daughter's graduation to drive the bus for the senior-adults spring foliage tour. "I can't come, Honey. They're depending on me to be there." I ask you, was he being led by the Holy Spirit or by his fleshly craving to be needed? Incidently, this young woman was into an affair less than a year later...seeking male acceptance.

I think of another man of God, this one a layman. For years he wouldn't come home after work until he had won at least one soul to Christ. Many people were won to Christ—except in his own house. I love this man and his family, but he made a tragic mistake. My dear brother, that price is too high to pay.

Here's another principle for husbands, drawn from Christ's relationship with His Bride…

## 4. HE LIVES THAT SHE MIGHT REACH HER FULL POTENTIAL

**Anabel:** Once again, let's put this on the practical level. *Husband, please be aware of me.*

As you have already come to see through our testimonies, Bill and I were not meeting each other's needs in the early years of our marriage. I want to share with you an episode that could have resulted in disaster.

### Playing a Dangerous Game

My story begins very innocently, at church. Our young married couples met together on Sunday evening, and on this particular Sunday night I had been asked to present a small part on the program. When I finished, I went back and sat down by a young man whom I'll call Don.

Don leaned over and whispered to me, "You enjoy doing things like that, don't you?"

I looked at him and said, "Why, yes. How did you know that?" (That's the performer in me, remember?)

Don said something that every woman loves to hear from a man: "Oh, I think I understand you." A man who understood me or was even interested in trying to understand me…I liked that. I wasn't getting understanding at home.

So with that small exchange, I began the womanly process of manipulation. When we would gather for church after our meeting, I would always arrange it so we would sit by Don and his wife. He didn't mind. We were playing a game.

I began evaluating his relationship with his wife. If she

were talking to me and Don entered into the conversation, her whole countenance would change, and she would be gruff and hateful with him. I never shall forget the night we were having a spaghetti supper at our house. I was standing by the stove, stirring the meat sauce. She was standing there talking with me. Don came up and slipped his arms around her waist. She flung them off and said, "Get away from me! You bother me!" You can easily see that Don was not getting his needs met, I was not getting my needs met, and we were embarking on an exciting new adventure together.

Don was very *aware* of me. I made all of my own clothes. I could work on a dress for weeks and even have Bill check the hemline, but still he would not notice enough to say anything nice about it *or* me. But, I could always count on Don.

**Bill:** Good ol' Don. You could always count on good ol' Don. That boy had a heart of gold.

**Anabel:** He would see me at church and say, "Hey, you have on a new dress. It's very becoming."

## Approaching the Danger Zone

I needed the attention, but it all came to a screeching halt one Sunday evening. Don and I were walking by ourselves over to the church building. (Bill didn't care where I walked or who I walked with. He was with a group of people telling his "funnies," and they were laughing at him. I didn't laugh at Bill. Nothing he did was funny. Bill hurt.) Don said to me, with a very intimate tone in his voice, "You look so pretty tonight, Anabel."

Women can recognize an intimate overture, and I didn't want that. I wanted attention, not intimacy. So, in an effort to lighten a heavy scene I said, "Oh, Don, you just see me on Sunday when I've really tried to look my best. You should see me some Monday."

He said, "I'd like to. May I?"

The game was over for me. I didn't want to go any further. But Don found another woman who was hurting as badly as he was hurting, and two marriages ended in tragic divorces.

## "That's My Favorite Color on You!"

I really do want to wear my hair the way my husband likes it, but how am I ever going to know unless he says to me, "I love your hair that way." I want to dress for him, to please him, but I won't know what he likes if he never notices me and says, "That's my favorite color on you." As a woman, I need that kind of attention, and I need to get it from my husband—not some other man.

**Bill:** Now guys, Sgt. Sin may be "saying" to you, "Well, I'm just not that way. I don't care how she wears her hair or what color blouse she wears." Hey, brother, pick a color!

That's all flesh, man. The old sin nature in you has died, and you are a brand new model. Christ is now your Life. Will He be able to make comments about your wife's hair through you if you'll wiggle your lips and believe He is doing it? Of course. But, you must come to the end of yourself and your fleshly ways if it's ever going to happen. Do it, bro. Three years from now you won't believe the change that will have taken place in you.

## How Long Has It Been...?

**Anabel:** A phone call came early one morning from a woman who related a story that I've heard time and time again. She said, "Anabel, a 'Don' came into my life, but I didn't get out when he asked for intimacy. Now I'm in an affair and it has destroyed my family. Oh Anabel, what can I do? I never intended for it to escalate to this point, but I so needed the man's tenderness and attention...."

How long has it been since you have said to your wife, "You look so pretty tonight, Sweetheart"? How long since you've noticed her hair on the day when she comes home from the beauty shop? How long since you have told her just how much you appreciate all of the things that she does to make herself attractive for just you? How long has it been?

"Husbands, love your wives...."

# A New Beginning — Right Now!

*In our own strength and resources,*
*being successfully married is impossible!*
*But, with Christ living through each*
*of you, a truly great future is*
*ahead for you and your marriage!*

# Chapter Fourteen

**A**nabel: Both of us are people watchers, and as the years have come and gone, we have heard and seen stories unfold all around us. Dramas about love and marriage are acted out before our eyes. Perhaps we are more aware of stories like these because of our interest in couples, and we hope that by sharing some of them with you, you'll begin to see how marriage looks through the eyes of Christ.

## Sticks and Stones

**Bill:** "Husbands, love your wives, and do not be harsh with them" (Colossians 3:19 RSV). It is unacceptable for a man to hit his wife; though I've not done that, I sadly acknowledge that many husbands do. So instead, some men lash out at them with harsh words. Now *that* I am guilty of.

The old adage, "Sticks and stones may break my bones but words will never harm me" is not true. If the lacerations made by thoughtless and cruel remarks from husbands and wives were visible, we would see gaping, bloody, festering wounds which never have the opportunity to heal. Not one of us is impervious to the pain of verbal abuse.

Can you imagine Christ verbally abusing His bride? No, that's not possible because…

## 5. HE DEDICATED HIMSELF TO HER THAT SHE MIGHT BE PURE THAT ALL OF HER IMPERFECTIONS MIGHT BE COVERED OVER BY HIS LOVE

**Anabel:** That is one of my favorite phrases of all the truths we've learned concerning the way Christ loves His Bride: *He covered over all her imperfections with His love.* How does this apply on a practical level in marriage? How about this? "Dear husband, please don't continually point out my mistakes to me. Please don't be harsh with me.…"

I had taken some materials to a little Mom and Pop print shop in Missouri, and they were to be done on the following Thursday afternoon. On Wednesday I was in the neighborhood so I thought I'd stop by and see if they were ready. The wife wasn't quite sure: "Just a minute, Anabel, and let me check with my husband."

Apparently, he didn't know (or didn't care) that his voice would carry over the pressroom noise to the front of the shop, because when she asked him about my materials, he let her know in no uncertain terms that the printing was not ready and that "any dummy" should have known that! And once he had started chewing her out, he decided to do a real good job of it and threw in a few more choice words.

I heard it all and felt terrible for having caused her such humiliation. She didn't come right back; she was doing what we wives who have suffered such treatment from our husbands call "regaining our composure." When she reappeared, her mascara was smeared, and she was holding her bottom lip between her teeth.

*Oh, husband, please do not be harsh with me....*

## "Can't You Read, Woman?"

I was in the grocery store rushing around and had no intention of eavesdropping on the couple in front of me. I had noticed them earlier, and because of the way they were dressed, I don't believe the following interaction was due to a lack of funds in the grocery account. We were walking down the vegetable aisle. The woman was filling their basket; he was pushing it. She picked up a bunch of radishes and put them in the cart.

"Can't you tell those things are pithy? Put 'em back!" he barked.

She put them back. They went on down the aisle, where she picked up a head of lettuce.

"Can't you read, woman? We don't need that stuff at that price!"

She put the lettuce back. They went on to the bacon, and she put a couple of pounds into the basket. I won't tell you what he said then.

*Oh, husband, please don't be harsh with me....*

## "Can't You Do Anything Right?"

A woman I know who is my same age was valedictorian of her graduating class in California just as I was at dear ol' Poteau, OK. High. Her achievement was much more of an honor in that there were over three thousand students in her high school....I was one of 65 high school graduates. She married one of the outstanding young men in her class. You might assume, "Well, that must have been a very successful marriage with two such fine people." Let me remind you: that talented young woman had been patterned in the world system to be strong, a performer, a perfectionist, and super sensitive—just like I was.

And that young man had been patterned, too, to be strong, a leader, threatened in his masculinity and verbal. As a couple, they started out very much the way Bill and I did.

That woman is not giving seminars or writing books on victorious Christian living today. She isn't even in her home. She is in an institution, and that vocabulary that won her the coveted award of valedictorian of her class has been reduced to two words..."yes" and "no." (She's heavily medicated.)

One year she came home for Christmas and because she wanted so badly to be a part of the festivities, she dressed herself (a major, laborious undertaking) and spent the day in the kitchen helping to prepare the Christmas dinner.

On Christmas evening, after all the preparations had been made, she put on a lovely gown and sat down with her family for supper. Something went amiss at the table, and feeling responsible as the hostess, she moved to correct the wrong. As she did, her sleeve caught the glass of water at her side, spilling it across the table. Do you know what her husband said to her?

He said the same thing that he began saying to her in their first little honeymoon apartment. He had said it many different ways, but the message was always the same.

He'd said it over and over and over until she finally believed him. That evening at the Christmas dinner table—that evening that she had worked so hard to make "special" for her husband and family, he said to her, "Can't you do anything right?"

Oh, husband, please don't do this to me....I am not emotionally equipped to handle such harshness. I realize that I frustrate you, and you get angry with me at times, but don't destroy me. You are to love me. Teach me. Be patient with me. Dedicate yourself to me. Let your love cover all my imperfections. Jesus says, *Above all, keep fervent in your love for one another, because love covers a multitude of sins* (1 Peter 4:8).

**Bill:** I am so grateful to God that He has shown me how to stop verbally mistreating my wife. How heartbreaking it would be if Christ treated us, His wife, the church, the way I treated mine for so long.

I pray that He shows my brother, who is reading these words with such a hungry heart, that only by choosing to pick up the cross "daily" and letting Christ live through him will he ever be able to experience victory over his flesh. When you and I "pick up our cross daily" we lose all our rights. We become servants.

Maybe the most sobering of all the ways Christ loves His Bride is this...

## 6. HE GAVE HIS LIFE FOR HER

The kind of sacrifice Christ made for every one of us—His Bride—is beyond our understanding, much less our ability to accomplish. It is a far smaller sacrifice, but an important one, for husbands to give our wives our time. Time is life on this planet. And by spending time with my wife, in a significant way I am giving my life for her.

## All Smiles and Packages

**Anabel:** The mall was rather crowded, folks shoulder-ing bags, dragging children, walking arm in arm—all oblivious to the angry-looking man who sat stiff and nervous on the bench in front of Hastings Records. His anger seethed at the passersby.

After a few moments his wife arrived, all smiles and packages. He stood up, enraged, and pointed to his watch. "You were supposed to be back here ten minutes ago! You could at least try to be on time. I expect you to be consid-erate of me. I didn't want to come in the first place! But no, you had to drag me on your damned shopping trip! And from the look of those packages, you've spent all of my money on yourself! Let's go."

*Spend time with me....*

## ...White Linen and Candlelight

Another little drama happened on Saturday night. The couple was out on the town. She had planned it all, a table for two in a quiet restaurant...flickering candles, a clean white cloth. It should have been enough to warm the heart of anyone. How she had anticipated this evening, doing her nails, hoping her hair would be just right for the occa-sion, fretting over what dress to wear so she would look her best for her "date."

All in the world she wanted was to prolong every pre-cious moment of this special evening out with the man she loved. She giggled, trying to make a light remark as she smiled at him and whispered, "Honey, don't eat so fast. You're going to be nearly finished before I even get my potato buttered."

An emotional bomb went off, and we, along with any-one within ten feet of them, could hear every word of his reply. "Well, if you think I'm going to sit here and dilly-dally around while you pick at your food until mine gets cold, you've got another thing coming! This was all your idea! I didn't want to come in the first place!"

Silence. He finished his steak, then ordered and ate his dessert. Without any further communication, they left, half of her meal still there where she had left it after the explosion. Behind them was the quiet little restaurant with flickering candles and clean white cloths on the tables.

*Spend time with me....*

## He Bought the Farm

**Bill:** Jane was fortyish, not the sort of woman who would turn every head, but an attractive lady nonetheless. She was having an affair and was planning to leave her husband and teenage sons as soon as her lover's divorce was final.

Jim, her husband, had been reared in extreme poverty. On one occasion things had been so bad that they had nothing in the house to eat but cornstarch. His mom had tried to make soup from it, but it was simply inedible. Jim vowed that he'd never be hungry again.

When Jane left him, Jim was working three jobs in an effort to pay off the farm, which he insisted God had "led him to buy." He had not taken her out for dinner in over ten years. "We need to get our farm paid off."

He frequently told his family that he was sacrificing his all for them, but Jane and the boys just as regularly told him they hated the farm with a passion and had never wanted to move to the country in the first place. His insensitivity caused Jane's sexual desire to sink to zero until she finally ceased to respond to his advances altogether.

It was at this point that Jim figured they had a marriage problem and was motivated to solve it. He decided that if Jane could get a job, the extra income would enable them to clear the farm mortgage that much sooner. This, he reasoned, would get her out of the house more and relieve the pressure. She took a job as a waitress during the night shift.

One rainy evening, a man came into the little diner where Jane worked, took a seat in his regular booth, and ordered a cup of coffee. He and Jane were alone in the restaurant, and although she was going about her duties, she was feeling lonely and melancholy. He picked up on it.

"What's the matter, Jane? You seem down."

"Oh, no. I'm fine."

"Aw, come on. I can tell you aren't yourself."

"It would take all night for me to tell you my life history. You don't have time for that."

"I'll take the time. Come on over and sit down. I'll buy the coffee and you spill the problems. The boss won't mind if you take a little break. Maybe I can help."

And so she did…and he did.… This was the man Jane was having the affair with…while Jim was paying off his farm.

*Spend time with me.…*

## Our Crow's Nest

**Anabel:** I still don't know just what the ingredients were that turned that rainy, blustery, chilly day in San Diego into such a lovely afternoon, but it was unforgettable. We had a layover, and instead of sitting in the airport, we took a city bus down to a village on the harbor. It was raining lightly, so we ran from store to store perusing the shelves. I bought some candles, and that was the extent of our purchases. We happened into a bookstore that had a loft where you could sit and have hot drinks and cookies. We browsed through the books, then took a cozy secluded table with a view of the bay and sipped our hot chocolate.

That's it. No thick, juicy steaks. No Hyatt Regency. No long-stemmed red roses. No surf. Just the two of us... together.

Thanks, sweet husband. You made something that could have been tedious and boring very special by simply spending time with me.

## Six Ways Christ Loves His Bride

In case our six points slipped past you in the midst of our stories and suggestions, we want you to have one last look at the model Christ has given husbands for loving their wives. Here is the example He sets for husbands as he loves His Bride:

1. Jesus longs for her to know just how much He loves her.
2. She is His consuming desire.
3. Every word, every action brings honor and expresses His devotion to her.
4. He lives that she might reach her full potential.
5. He dedicated himself to her that she might be pure, that all of her imperfections might be cov ered over by His love.
6. He gave His life for her.

Perhaps as a husband, it seems impossible to apply those ideas to the practical matter of daily living within your marriage.

Perhaps as a wife, you feel you've given all you can, and you have no more to offer your husband.

Perhaps both of you believe that your marriage is a lost cause—an impossible situation.

In one sense, you're right. In our own strength and resources, being successfully married is impossible! But, with Christ living through each of you, a truly great future is ahead for you and your marriage! He wants to give you both a new beginning—right now.

## Ready for a New Beginning?

**Bill:** I'm sure you have some questions you're going to have to work through; that's to be expected. You probably have a good idea by now of just where your own personal problems lie. I hope you'll remember that the secret to living the Christian life is not discovered through rules, regulations, and concepts; instead, Christ as your Life is your "secret;" He has replaced your old "lord-of-the-ring" life with Himself *as* Life.

To experience Christ as Life requires a total, sellout commitment. Stepping out, giving up all control, and placing yourself totally in His hands can be frightening. But the choice is yours. He will not impose His will upon you. He is totally committed to you, and you can either walk away or commit yourself totally to Him.

Would you like to take that first step toward a whole new approach to life?

Would you like to start all over again with new hope?

Would you like to believe that you're doing something positive about the relationships in your life?

Would you like to try again?

If your answer is "Yes, I would," then slip away to a private place and read the following words as your prayer of commitment.

*My Jesus,*
*I don't understand all of this completely*
*(I doubt anyone does),*
*but I believe that when You died at Calvary,*
*The old "I" was in You and I died in You.*
*When You were buried in that forsaken tomb,*
*I, too, was buried;*
*and when You were raised, I was re-created*
*as a new person in You…I was born again.*
*There is only One Person who can live the Christian*
*life—You—and You are now my Life.*
*I offer myself to You to express Your Life through me,*
*and I want You to start in my own home with those You*
*have given to me, with those who are most precious to me.*
*Jesus, I take my first step forward*
*and I rest in the certainty of You. Amen.*

## A Note from Bill and Anabel:

*Lifetime Guarantee*, by Bill and *The Confident Woman*, by Anabel (both by Harvest House Publishers) each go into great detail to help you appropriate the truth in Colossians 3:3: "For you have died and your life is hidden with Christ in God." Note that your true life is "hidden" and must be experienced by simply stepping out on faith that it's true.[1]

God bless you in your pilgrimage, dear ones. You're going to make it. God says, "...and stand he will, for the Lord is able to make him stand" (Romans 14:4).

---

[1] We also have audio and video tapes to assist you.

## CONCERNING LIFETIME GUARANTEE, INC.

Bill and Anabel Gillham minister through Lifetime Guarantee, Inc. LGI proclaims the dual truths of the believer's true identity in Christ and Christ expressing His Life through the believer as *the* keys to victorious Christian living.

LGI produces the nationally syndicated radio program "Lifetime Guarantee" and conducts live seminars across the United States. We welcome invitations to speak.

For a free catalog of teaching materials, or to obtain LGI's free monthly Ministry Letter containing articles on victorious Christian living as well as the most recent speaking itinerary, call 1-800-328-6662; or write to Lifetime Guarantee, 4100 International Plaza, Suite 520, Ft. Worth, Texas 76109.

## ABOUT THE AUTHORS

Dr. Bill and Anabel Gillham have worked with people since their first years as school teachers. Bill was an Associate Professor of Psychology at Southeastern Oklahoma State University until 1975, when he left the educational system to become a Christian counselor.

It was then that he and Anabel began lecturing on "Victorious Christian Living," a seminar they have presented worldwide through Lifetime Guarantee, Inc., of Ft. Worth, Texas.

The Gillhams, native Oklahomans, reside in Gransbury, Texas. They have four sons: Pres, Mason, Will, and Wade, and live at Pecan Plantation with their dog, Bo.